Vygotsky on Education
PRIMER

This book is part of the Peter Lang Education list.
Every volume is peer reviewed and meets
the highest quality standards for content and production.

PETER LANG
New York • Washington, D.C./Baltimore • Bern
Frankfurt • Berlin • Brussels • Vienna • Oxford

Robert Lake

Vygotsky on Education
PRIMER

PETER LANG
New York • Washington, D.C./Baltimore • Bern
Frankfurt • Berlin • Brussels • Vienna • Oxford

Library of Congress Cataloging-in-Publication Data
Lake, Robert.
Vygotsky on education primer / Robert Lake.
p. cm. — (Peter Lang primers)
Includes bibliographical references and index.
1. Educational psychology. 2. Learning, Psychology of.
3. Cognition and culture. 4. Vygotskii, L. S. (Lev Semenovich), 1896–1934.
5. Teaching. I. Title.
LB1051.L17   370.15—dc23   2012002666
ISBN 978-1-4331-1355-0 (paperback)
978-1-4539-0763-4 (e-book)

Bibliographic information published by **Die Deutsche Nationalbibliothek.**
Die Deutsche Nationalbibliothek lists this publication in the "Deutsche
Nationalbibliografie"; detailed bibliographic data is available
on the Internet at http://dnb.d-nb.de/.

The paper in this book meets the guidelines for permanence and durability
of the Committee on Production Guidelines for Book Longevity
of the Council of Library Resources.

© 2012 Peter Lang Publishing, Inc., New York
29 Broadway, 18th floor, New York, NY 10006
www.peterlang.com

Printed in the United States of America

Contents

Introduction

"*Vygotsky left an impressive body of work that, as is the case with most geniuses, become[s] more modern as time goes by*" (Blanck, 1990, p. 31).

Who was the Russian psychologist Lev Vygotsky and is his work still relevant to educators in the 21st century? In what ways does his work converge with the field of progressive education in general and critical pedagogy in particular? These are some of the questions that provided the impetus to write this book as a part of the Peter Lang primer series along with *Critical Pedagogy* (2008), *Bakhtin* (2007), *Foucault and Education* (2005) and *John Dewey* (2006) to name a few related titles.

All of Vygotsky's contemporaries and present day scholars in psychology will attest to the fact that he was a genius and a forerunner to the field of cognitive psychology. However, he had many other interests as well, including poetry, theatre, fiction and

film. His unique and groundbreaking theories on the dialectical connections between thought and language are timeless and priceless contributions to all content areas of education. Before his untimely death at age 38 he had written or co-written 180 major works, transformed the practice of Soviet psychology from its behaviorist origins, and almost singlehandedly created what we now call the field of special education.

Even though he died almost 80 years ago, in many ways his life work is even more relevant and significant to the field of education today than in the 20th century. This book gives centrality to Vygotsky's emphasis on the role of the cultural and historical context in learning and challenges theories that emphasize a universalistic view of learning through fixed biologically determined stages of development. In this present time of undue preoccupation with standardized outcomes and the corporatization of schooling, Vygotsky's most important ideas about education need to be freshly considered.

The book opens with a snapshot of Vygotsky bursting on the public scene at a national conference on Soviet psychology. From the beginning of his career until his death 14 years later, he challenged the status quo by imagining and acting against the grain of given orthodoxy. Particular attention is given to the cultural-historical context of Vygotsky's life as the shaping dynamic behind his views on education. This is followed by an overview of his two most popular ideas: the zone of proximal development and the development of thinking and speech as a means of empowerment. Another chapter introduces the readers to Vygotsky's views of both critical and creative imagination in the formation of personal agency and in creative collaboration. In Chapter Five Lake explores the convergence between Vygotsky's work and critical pedagogy through a framework provided by Joseph Schwab's notion of the four commonplaces of curriculum—milieu, teacher, subject matter, and learner. This chapter also provides an overview of present day

practices and practitioners that clearly reflect and build upon Vygotsky's work in a wide array of international and multicultural settings across all age levels. Applications to current practices from an expansive range of sources help provide clarity and relevance to diverse audiences. The primer format maintains the essence of Vygotsky's work in language that is accessible to all students of education.

CHAPTER ONE

Lev Vygotsky in Cultural-Historical Context

On January 6th, 1924 an unusually lucid and striking young delegate named Lev Vygotsky made his national debut by addressing the second All-Union Congress on Psychoneurology that was held in St. Petersburg, Russia. His presentation is described by his daughter Gita Vygodskaya in an oft-repeated story from Vygotsky's colleague Alexander Luria.

According to those present it was about a very "hot" topic of the day: "Methods of reflexological and psychological investigation"* and listeners were impressed first by the manner of presentation. The speech was smooth, crystal clear, and very log-

* All short citations will be listed in order of appearance in the text, at the end of each paragraph in which they were cited. Many ideas in Chapters 3–5 are drawn from my dissertation completed in 2006 at Georgia Southern University under the title: *A Curriculum of Imagination Beyond Walls of Standardization.*

ical. In his hand the presenter had a small piece of paper. When Alexander Luria approached him after the presentation, he was surprised to find the paper blank. But most surprising was the fact that this speaker, for whom this was the first time in front of such a qualified audience, was not afraid to (as A. Luria put it) "go against the tide." (Vygodskaya, 1995, p. 111)

Perhaps the 28-year-old genius did not want to appear to be too far out of the range of "normal" by not using any notes at all. Whatever his reasons were, his life's work far transcended the status quo during his short 38 years of life and is just as relevant today as it was during his lifetime.

Growing up in Czarist Russia

It is richly instructive to consider how Vygotsky's life was situated in the socio-historical context of the collapse of Czarist Russia and in the formative years of the Russian Revolution and the rise of European Fascism. As he lived through this extraordinary time period, his views on the profound influence of culture and history in shaping the psychology of learning were formed. Rene van der Veer summarizes the tumultuous period of Vygotsky's short life. "He certainly experienced several revolutions, World War I, the German and Ukrainian occupations, the civil war, famine, and political repression." Lev Semyonovich Vygotsky was born into a Jewish family on November 5th, 1896 in a small town in Belorussia called Orsha. Early in his childhood, his father received a new job at the United Bank of Gomel as a department leader so his family relocated to be near this place of employment. In Czarist Russia, Jews were not allowed to own land and were forbidden to live anywhere except a specific area of a city or village called the **pale of settlement**. (van der Veer, 2007, p. 23)

Pale of Settlement

This was the allotted land in Czarist Russia where Jews were allowed to live.

Czarist Russian society was designed to see to it that all people stayed in their natural station in life. Nobility and clergy got all the privileges. For Vygotsky, the second child of eight in a Russian-Jewish family, this meant his station was the pale of settlement. When Lev Vygotsky was seven years old he witnessed a **pogrom** and his father was summoned to court as a witness. Jewish culture and religion posed a threat to the Czarist regime. Jews could not own their own land, were not permitted to speak Hebrew, and were greatly restricted in terms of settlement, travel, and occupation. Jews were granted citizenship status but were portrayed as oppressors of Slavic Christians. The most brutal expressions of anti-Semitism were the pogroms.

Local gang members, laborers, and even police officials targeted Jewish communities for looting, rape, murder, and destruction. While Czarist authorities didn't plan the pogroms, they sanctioned them. (Lowe, 2009)

Pogrom
a Russian word that literally means "destruction" which took on the meaning of an organized mass attack against a community of Jews that was either directly or indirectly officially sanctioned.

But residents of the pale of settlement in Gomel did not just passively accept all of the effects of marginalization. In 1903, "after a full-scale pogrom, the Jewish residents of Gomel fought back and eventually defeated their attackers." Kozulin explains this event in further detail, and I include the account here because it is certain to have made an impression on the seven-year-old Vygotsky. (Newman & Holtzman, 1993, p. 156)

In the fall of 1903 a trivial incident at the farmers' market in Gomel triggered a full-scale pogrom of the Jewish businesses and dwellings themselves; Gomel's Jews resisted and on some occasions defeated their attackers. As a result a large number of Jews were brought to trial for allegedly assaulting the Russians. The trial soon became the setting for a major confrontation between democratic forces demanding full rights for minorities and pro-government groups who were eager to place the blame

on the Jews. Vygotsky's father, Simha (Semion in Russian) was called as a witness to testify about the general atmosphere in the town on the eve of the pogrom. Vygodsky Sr. offered his opinion that after the famous Kishenev pogrom that had occurred earlier in 1903 it had become clear that the authorities would not defend the Jews and that pogroms would be perpetuated with impunity. He also elaborated on the psychological reasons for the heightened tension between Russians and Jews, suggesting that the growing awareness on the part of Jews of their human rights seemed to be offending some Russians: As long as Jews did not talk about this, all was good, but when they started to consider themselves as people like others and talk about their human dignity, the attitude toward them has changed. (1990, pp. 13–14)

For the young Vygotsky, all of these events helped shape his consciousness of human rights and his lifetime engagement in the work of cultivating **personal agency** by not accepting events passively but to acting upon the world as a participant in the unfolding of history. We will delve into the concept of agency in greater detail later in this chapter in a discussion of the people who shaped Vygotsky's thinking.

Personal agency
This refers to the personal ability to take charge of one's own learning, life and unique circumstances.

According to Alex Kozulin's account, "the family appears to have been well respected in the town, being involved in some public endeavors such as the establishment of a library." Lev's mother was educated as a teacher but chose to use her education to enhance her own children's education by staying at home with them. (1990, p. 13) Vygotsky's daughter describes his home setting best:

There were eight children in the family, each a year and a half apart. Lev was the second; he had an older sister. The older children, with Lev no exception, helped the mother in the housework and cared for the younger ones. The family was very tightly-knit being united by common interests: his-

tory, literature, theater, and art. It was a family tradition to get together after the evening tea. By this time everyone was done with his or her activities, the father with business, mother with housework, and children with their school assignments. They then talked amongst themselves about whatever came to mind, or read aloud either classic novels or newly released ones. Both the parents and children valued this time of family closeness and spoke warmly of it for many years to come.

This tradition persisted when the children grew up and had their own families. I remember these conversations well, when some of us sat at the table and some near the warm stove. All the children were right there, but they never interrupted the adult conversations or readings. We just sat quietly, played with our toys, and listened to the adults. None of us was forced to be in the room, but I never could remember a time when anyone left the room during these gatherings, and I remember being upset when my mother finally sent me up to my room to sleep. If my father came home alone he always joined in; if he brought home a colleague from work, he stayed for the tea but then went to work.

But let's return to Gomel. According to recollection of Lev's sisters, my aunts, the family life style was very modest. Besides the school uniform the children had only one set of clothes each, which the mother made herself. But despite that, there was always money for books: they were purchased often and the household had a large collection of classics. The children were often taken to play productions: in those days Gomel was often visited by talented actors. In this way the children, since the earliest age, were exposed to literature and performing arts.

Lev was growing up as a sociable boy. His peers were drawn to him, and he was often surrounded by friends. They all shared his interests such as stamp collecting, chess, and, by their own admission, reading of adventure novels. During the summer he spent time on the river, swimming or taking his sisters and friends in a boat. In those years he be-

come interested in Esperanto and learned the language on his own.

He received his elementary education at home, studying independently and having a tutor for consultation. He passed an exam for the first 5 years of grade school and entered into a private all boys secondary school. Lev was a steady consistent student, doing equally well in all subjects, and the teachers often commented on his superb abilities. His math teacher predicted him a brilliant future as a mathematician, his literature teacher—as a philologist. Already in those early years he stood out in his breadth and depth of interest. All his learning was marked by seriousness and maturity. Of all his subjects he most preferred literature and philosophy: these were objects of his fascination and involvement. He knew the Russian classics well but was also interested in contemporary Russian and foreign literature.

Although far advanced in his abilities and level of knowledge, he, according to his schoolmates, never acted cocky, or condescending. It was not in his character to do so. He carried himself in a conservative manner, and was always ready to help out anyone who needed it. He willingly and patiently explained difficult topics, and his friends greatly respected him for it. This willingness to help out everyone stayed with him all his life: his colleagues recalled how he often helped a friend for hours at times, ignoring fatigue. (Vygodskaya, 1995, pp. 106–108)

All of these experiences laid the foundation for Vygotsky's' views on the value of learning communities and what we shall later discuss in detail about the zone of proximal development. Suffice it to say at this point that this concept is not a static system of measuring predetermined levels of development or a geographical place in a classroom where the chairs are placed in circles, but to quote directly from Vygotsky: "It is the distance between the actual developmental level as determined by independent problem solving, and the level of potential development as determined through problem solving under adult guidance or in collaboration with more capable peers." In this book, we will devote a whole chapter to this notion and give numerous examples from present practices, but it is important to note throughout this chapter that Vygotsky created zones of proximal development wherever he found himself throughout his entire life. (1978, p. 86)

By his middle teenage years "Vygotsky became known as the 'little professor' because of his passion for learning along with a philosophical orientation." Also as a teen, "he often led student discussions on intellectual matters." One of the activities he and his friends engaged in during this period was the reenactment of historical trials and imagined debates. This activity became the seedbed for his theories of the value of play and performance in the dynamic process of learning and development that we will discuss at length in this book. (Wertsch, 1985, p. 4)

In these formative years young Lev became passionate about philosophy, literature, drama and poetry. One of Vygotsky's childhood friends would later recall that "literature, especially his favorite poetry, always gave him much solace in life and always engaged his attention." In fact it was literature and the arts that comprised the first love of his scholarly life. This is important to note when we consider Vygotsky's role as one of the primary pathfinders in the field of cultural-historical approaches to educational psychology. (Dobkin, quoted in Wertsch, 1985, p. 4.

By the time Vygotsky was 17 he graduated from secondary school with a gold medal for his academic achievement. Normally this would have assured him a placement in the University of Moscow, but because of the anti-Semitic quota system that was in place in Czarist Russia, the only way that Lev could be admitted was through a lottery drawing. Again his good friend Semyon Dobkin recounts the drama of this moment:

The news seemed so monstrous to me that I replied quite sincerely: "If they don't admit you to the University it will be a terrible injustice. I am sure they'll let you in. Wanna bet?" Vygotsky, who was a great better, smiled and stretched out his hand. We wagered for a good book. He did not make a single mistake on his final exams and received a gold medal. At the insistence of his parents, he applied to the medical department which was considered most suitable because it guaranteed a modest but secure future. True, Vygotsky was more interested in the humanities, but what were his options? The history and philology departments were out because they trained mainly secondary school teachers, and Jews were not allowed to be government employees in tsarist Russia. And the law department, too, generally turned out court officials, although it also opened the opportunity to become an attorney. And then the incredible happened: late in August, the Vygodskys* received a cable from their friends in Moscow telling them that Lev had been enrolled at the University by the draw. On the same day, he presented me with a volume of Bunin's poetry inscribed "To Senya in memory of a lost bet." I don't think anyone was ever so happy about losing a bet. (Levitin, 1982, pp. 28–29)

Once he was assured a seat at Moscow University, Vygotsky wanted to study the humanities since his main interests were in "theatre, literature and philosophy," but "this area of study would lead to the field of teaching, which was denied to him because of his religion at that time." The only alternative was to enroll as a medical student. Later he transferred to the field of law. While he was attending Moscow University he was also studying at

---

* Vygotsky replaced the "d" in his name with a "t" in the early 1920s because he believed that his name derived from the name of the village of Vygotovo where the family had its roots (ibid., p. 11).

an unaccredited institution called "Shaniavsky People's University. This school provided Vygotsky with a rich intellectual environment of collegiality." (Blanck, 1990, p. 33; Wink & Putney, 2003, p. xix)

> Created in 1906 by Alfons Shaniavsky after the Ministry of Education expelled from Moscow's Imperial University most of the students who had participated in an anti-czarist revolt. In protest about a hundred leading scholars left the university . . . as a result, the highest intellects in Moscow gathered there. Vygotsky obtained a solid foundation in history, philosophy, and psychology and pursued studies in literature which continued to be his primary interest.

During his time as a student in higher education, Vygotsky made outstanding contributions to the field of literary criticism. In fact, many believe "it was among his best work, although it has since been lost." One such essay he wrote in 1916 was also one of his thesis papers on Shakespeare's *Hamlet*. He had actually started writing this piece while still a young student but "he did not show it to anyone. It was his most closely guarded secret. The essay was eventually published as a supplement to the second edition of *The Psychology of Art*." (Wink & Putney, 2003, p. xix; Dobkin, 1982, p. 16)

Perhaps the reason that Vygotsky invested so much thought into the story of *Hamlet* is because even as a teenager, he could already sense so much of his life was a tragedy. In fact, from that point on his life became more and more tragic until it was cut short by terminal illness. Kozulin comments on this: "His preoccupation with the theme of death, which revealed itself so poignantly in the essay on *Hamlet*, had very real roots in his own life. There was a history of tuberculosis in Vygotsky's family and he experienced one of his first attacks in 1920." The disease later caused his premature death at age 38. (1990, pp. 64–65)

Yet unlike many scholars from the early 20th century, instead of his work losing relevance after his death, it has become more and more significant as theories of behaviorism and operant conditioning were challenged in the second half of the 20th century. As we enter the second decade of the 21st century, Vygotsky's views of development are especially cogent against the backdrop of "performance standards" and learning objectives and highly scripted curricula containing state and federally approved "official knowledge." Vygotsky's work has also found new significance in the area of interdisciplinary studies because he himself was passionate about art, poetry, literature and philosophy in addition to his work in psychology. (Apple, 1993)

Shortly after Vygotsky graduated from both universities in 1917, he returned to his family home in Gomel. A few months later the entire country was thrown into utter social, economic and political upheaval which dramatically brought about the end of Czarist Russia.

> World War I brought severe chaos and deprivation to the Russian people, which in turn, sparked uprising and the Russian Revolution. "Peace, bread, and land" became the slogan of the day, and civil war continued to ravish the people with injustice, starvation, and violence. Still, what the revolution accomplished was to break down the barriers between classes. For the first time in Russia, people were able to choose their own careers without regard to their social origins. Young people threw their whole being into the new movement because they recognized the opportunities that it offered. (Lowe, 2009)

According to his daughter, Vygotsky fully embraced the Soviet Revolution as an active participant. She stated in an interview that, "He heartily accepted the revolution because it had abolished the laws discriminating against the Jews." To further support this testimony, the biographer Guillermo Blanck claims

to have in his possession a copy of "his *carnet* of deputy of the Soviet of Frunze district of Moscow." The ironic part of this is that from that time into the not too distant future, the leaders of the communist party would purge all of Vygotsky's writings from every public library and education center because his ideas threatened Stalin's authoritarian policies. (Vygodskaya quoted in Lowe, 2009; 1990, p. 35)

After the revolution of October 1917, Vygotsky returned home and had to help take care of sick members of his family. Vygotsky's daughter provides us a rare glimpse into the tragic situation on the home front in a few words that speak volumes about Vygotsky's capacity to care for and support others.

> The family was also going through a difficult time. Lev had two sick relatives on his hands: his mother recovering from a bout with tuberculosis, and his younger brother who also contracted the disease, and whose condition was deemed critical. The young boy needed constant care; Lev was his nanny and cared for him until the boy died before his 14th birthday. His mother, stricken by grief, fell ill again, and Lev once again had to care for her. Before the end of the year, another tragedy struck the family: Lev's second brother died of typhoid fever, and so ended his first year back in Gomel. (Vygodskaya, 1995, p. 109)

The cold weather and lack of solid nutrition certainly must have been a factor that contributed to the family's dreadful health problems that eventually would terminally infect Vygotsky himself. Yet in spite of the grim and dire existence for countless families in Gomel in the post-revolutionary years, the city was a center for an avant-garde arts and culture movement, and Vygotsky was there in the very middle of all this activity, teaching and taking a leadership role in theatre activities. In addition he "initiated 'Literary Mondays' where new prose and poetry were discussed and was one of the founders of the magazine *Veresk*." (Blanck, 1990, p. 37)

Erudite Teacher of Culture and Literature

Erudite
Showing depth and breadth of learning and scholarship.

For the next seven years in Gomel he taught in a wide variety of settings ranging from "literature, aesthetics, philosophy, and Russian language in the newly opened vocational school and then psychology and logic in a local teachers college." Vygotsky was very well rounded in his scholarly pursuits. Van der Veer elaborates on the breadth of Vygotsky's erudition. (Vygodskaya, 1995, p. 110)

> (He) was not a bigoted intellectual who knew only his own favorite discipline and pet hypotheses. On the contrary, he was a man of immense culture who kept abreast of the recent developments in literature, drama, the fine arts and music. Above all, Vygotsky absorbed new theatre performances and the new poems and novels. (2007, p. 24)

Yet we must be clear that although his interests appear to be diffuse and only quasi-related on the surface, that for Vygotsky, they were all related in his quest for ways to connect learning and development to culture, history, language processes, psychopathology, cross-cultural inquiry, disability studies, physical labor, imagination, art and literature. Newman and Holtzman write that "it is the fields that are diverse: human existence is seamless. The compartmentalization of human existence creates the illusion that someone who lives and investigates its totality has a diversity of interests." (1993, p. 159)

By 1919 he contracted tuberculosis but showed amazing resilience for the next 15 years until his death. And in spite of his deteriorating health, his gifts as a teacher did not go unnoticed. His daughter found an announcement in a local paper that attested to this.

> In one of the local papers of that time I found an interesting announcement. The newspaper in conjunction with the local Department of Education was looking for a nominee as the best teacher of the

province. All were encouraged to send to the editor profiles of those teachers seemed to be the most worthy of that title. Lists of names were published once a week. Soon after, Lev Vygotsky's name appeared as the best teacher of the Gomel province. In one of the documents issued by the local Pedagogical Council, the significance of L. S. Vygotsky's work was highlighted as having: "... showed pedagogical tact, eagerness, and erudition in teaching. " (Vygodskaya, 1995, p. 110)

Lev Vygotsky married Rosa Noevna Smekhova in 1924 and had two daughters. Gita is one of the main sources of biography on Vygotsky. She was the older of the two and followed in her father's footsteps as an educational psychologist. "The younger daughter Asya was a specialist in biophysics. It is said that Rosa kept her spirits up during Vygotsky's illness, and she worked long days taking care of handicapped children after his death in 1934. Rosa died in 1979, and Asya died in 1985." (Wink & Putney, 2003, p. xx) *Gita herself died on July 13, 2010.* (Italics, mine)

Along with his wedding, another milestone in Vygotsky's life took place that year, which takes us back to the opening scene of this chapter, when Vygotsky gave his masterful presentation at the All-Union Congress on Psychoneurology in St. Petersburg in 1924. The presentation made such an impression on Konstantin Kornilov, director of the Institute of Psychology of Moscow, that he invited Vygotsky on the spot to join the institute as a research fellow. Vygotsky accepted the position and moved with his new bride to Moscow a few weeks later.

Vygotsky's Intellectual Roots

Because Vygotsky was such an exceptionally prolific reader and thinker with an extraordinary memory, it would be nearly impossible to trace the origin of

all the intellectual influences upon his thinking and writing. His colleague Luria reported that Vygotsky possessed a peculiar gift in speed reading because he "read diagonally" across the page. In addition to his first language, he spoke German, French, Hebrew, English, Esperanto and he also learned Greek and Latin (ibid.). He used these language skills to translate many scholarly works into Russian and "in that process of translation, he sort of went through, like a tunnel, their theory and ended up on the other end and found his own way of thinking about some of the concepts" (John-Steiner quoted in Lowe, 2009). Consequently we will look at just a few of the major influences in his writing that have a direct bearing on his views of education. (Luria quoted in Blanck, 1990, p. 33)

It is widely accepted and known by Vygotsky scholars that "most of his theoretical ideas came from Hegel, Marx and Spinoza" and that "when he is not reporting empirical studies, he admits this." The ideas of these three thinkers are all interrelated and build on each other to provide the background for Vygotsky's dialectical process of inquiry. (Langford, 2005, pp. 249; 173)

Spinoza (1632–1677)

Van der Veer highlights three areas in Spinoza's work that influenced Vygotsky. They are "intellectualism... monism or determinism and third is the use of intellectual tools." (n.d.), p. 90)

Intellectualism can be summarized as the view that humans do not have to be slaves to emotions when the intellect is aware of them. Vygotsky himself cites Spinoza on this. "Spinoza correctly stated, the knowledge of an emotion changes this emotion and changes it from a passive into an active state. (O)ur emotions act in a complex system with our state. Indeed it is this complex yet integral and holistic system where emotions are the servant of higher mental functions that Spinoza and Vygot-

sky depart from the dualistic split of mind and body that was generally accepted from Plato all the way up to Spinoza. (Vygotsky, 1982a, p. 125)

Monism as used by Spinoza and Vygotsky refers to the inward oneness of nature, mind and emotions. This view is important when we discuss the formation of Vygotsky's notion of higher levels of **consciousness** that arise out of the oneness of natural impulse with active exercise of the mind. Vygotsky wrote:

> (T)he mind is not, to use an expression of Spinoza, something beyond nature or a state within a state, it is part of nature itself, directly connected to the functions or higher organized matter of our brain. Like all other nature it was not created but evolved in a developmental process. (1982a, p. 137)

Spinoza refers to "intellectual tools for the controlling of one's own emotional behavior." In Vygotsky's work, tools are sign systems that create higher mental functions, and the prime example that he uses for this, of course, is language. For example, Braille is a tool for mediating touch and emotion with the development of thought. (van der Veer, n.d., p. 95)

Consciousness

self-awareness including the capacity to think, feel, form concepts, reflect on one's own thinking as well as creatively and critically imagine.

Hegel (1770–1831)

The influence of Hegel in both Vygotsky and Marx is quite complex and really requires a level of clarification beyond a short section in a primer. However there are a few main ideas that can be outlined that will help us as we consider Vygotsky's theory and practice of education. Kozulin provides a clear yet non-simplistic overview of Hegel's influences in Vygotsky's work: "The essence of history is the process of the self expression of Mind." The progress of history is only possible through conscious and deliberate practice. Only then are humans moving for the consciousness of freedom. (1990, p. 16)

Kozulin further elaborates on this. "Historical Development is not a straight ascending line, but a complex trajectory replete with detours and reversals" (ibid.). The dynamic movement of this trajectory provides us with the core definition of dialectical progress wherein seemingly opposing vantage points and contradictions exist within all non-static knowledge. This dynamic has been described in the thesis-antithesis-synthesis process, but Vygotsky would consider this too much a linear process. Kincheloe provides a clearer description of this dynamic when he says that "knowledge is not complete in and of itself. It is produced in a larger process and can never be understood outside of its historical development and its relationship to other information." In this astute summary, Kincheloe succinctly defines for us Hegel's view that knowledge is not static and fixed but exists in the particular cultural context of situated human consciousness. (Kozulin, 1990, 16; Kincheloe, 2008, p. 17)

Hegel and Vygotsky distinguish the natural animal aspect of life as existence which "coincides with its 'being'; human existence is realized in 'becoming.'" It is through activity and work in particular that humans reach self-consciousness. "Work therefore is a social, rather than a natural activity; it creates a non-natural, technical and at the same time humanized world." To Hegel and Vygotsky 'work' is connected to language; in fact, Hegel's view of history is that it is the sum of thinking and speaking. (We will go into this in greater detail in Chapter Three.) This notion of becoming is the essence of Vygotsky's notion of development. (Kozulin, 1990, pp. 16–17)

Marx (1818–1883)

Marx transformed Hegel's view of the dialectical development of history from one of idealist philosophy which says that history is comprised of the

Mechanical materialism

a static view of history that is void of the concept of development. In this view all matter is comprised of a system of mechanical bodies that "existed at the start of time and will exist at the end of time. The laws of motion and the way forces interact always remains the same" (Langford, 2005, p. 23)

Dialectical historical materialism

refers to Marx's notion that "a system of matter in motion may, as a result of the conflict of tendencies within itself develop new laws that were not there from the start." (Langford, 2005, p. 23) These changes create changes in societies that shape the way people think. (See end of chapter for example).

evolution of ideas, to a materialistic concept which maintains rather that history is governed "by the evolution of the productive forces." In fact both Marx and Engels used the following slogan a number of times in their writings "Marxism is Hegel turned on his head or rather on his feet." Nevertheless Marx made a clear distinction between **mechanical materialism** and **dialectical historical materialism**. (Langford, 2005, p. 25; Marx, quoted in Langford, 2005, p. 24)

Both Marx and Vygotsky believed that when "man interacts with nature and transforms it . . . nature also interacts with man and transforms his consciousness." Or as Vygotsky puts it "method is simultaneously prerequisite and product, the tool and the result of the study." This concept will be discussed further in Chapter Two when we explore the process of internalization in the zone of proximal development. (Gaardner, 1994, p. 397; Vygotsky, 1978, p. 65)

Vygotsky's Quest for a New Psychology

The focus of Vygotsky's scholarship shifted once he moved to Moscow and began his position as a research fellow in psychology. His office was in the basement of a section of the university library that housed books on philosophy and literature and Vygotsky made the most of these resources. It is intriguing but not surprising therefore that the first publication that he completed after accepting his new position was called *The Psychology of Art* (1925). Blanck suggests that Vygotsky's "real interest was in solving problems of art and culture that he turned to psychology in order to solve them and eventually was captured by it." There is ample evidence to confirm this from the simple fact that so much of his writing on psychology contains literary allusions

and quotations from poetry. This is another example of how Vygotsky was far ahead of his time in transgressing borders between disciplines as he looked for ways to understand the influence of culture and historical events on theories of knowledge. (1990, p. 38)

Yet clearly for Vygotsky there remained an emphasis on the psychology of pedagogy in all his work. Jerome Bruner goes so far as to say that Vygotsky's theories of development are all learning theories. In the context of Vygotsky's life history up to this period, this view follows a logical progression, since he had been a teacher for seven years up to that point (1987e, prologue, p. 1). Blanck cites two major voices in Vygotsky scholarship supporting this view when he writes:

> This opinion is supported by Moll...when he states that pedagogy is the essential route of Vygotsky's approach to psychology. Mecacci (1983) expresses a similar opinion. These affirmations are supported by the fact that seven of Vygotsky's first eight writings on psychology between 1922 and 1926 have to do with problems in education, such as methods of teaching literature, the use of translation in language comprehension, and the education of blind, deaf-mute, retarded, and physically handicapped children. (1990, p. 38)

However both these lines of inquiry into psychology—art and education—are inclusive in Vygotsky's quest for a new model of psychology that focused on consciousness in contrast to the primitive model that was built on neural reflexes and impulses and stimulus response methods of behaviorism. It is important to remember that at this point in history, psychology was still a relatively new discipline that, up until 1879, was still considered integral to the study of philosophy. So the contribution that Vygotsky made to the field in the early 20th century was revolutionary then and still continues to have relevance in this present climate of drill and skill "teaching for the test" emphasis in schools today. It is little wonder therefore that interest in his work is at an all-time high as teachers look for ways to move beyond standardized schooling and "teacher proof" curriculum that often serves to dumb down intellectual processes that lead to higher levels of thinking for both teachers and students. For Vygotsky advances in development and fuller degrees of consciousness were inseparable and were best identified in activity or motion, not in isolated, detached and decontextualized, multiple choice options. In summary, Kozulin states that "Vygotsky did not even take psychology to be the object of study, but rather he took it to be a tool with which to investigate culture and consciousness." (cited in Newman and Holzman, 1993, p. 30)

The specific areas of the early discipline of psychology that Vygotsky's work sought to challenge are summed up in Wink and Putney's summary of the del Rio and Alvarez (1995) article on the role of directivity in Vygotsky's legacy of psychology. "Vygotsky sought to address four major areas of reductionism in psychology: that of reduction to the rational, to the individual, to the internal, and to the innate." (2003, pp. xxi–xxii) The following is a paraphrase of their work.

- **Rational**. Vygotsky challenged the Cartesian notion that the mind could be objectively measured and could process thought without being influenced by feeling and subjective experiences. He took a full account of the value of emotion in consciousness and sought to incorporate play and performance in cultivating higher orders of thought and creativity. We will explore these issues more fully in Chapters Two and Three.
- **Individual**. During Vygotsky's lifetime, the prevailing view of psychology was almost completely focused on an individualistic view of the formation of thinking processes. Vygotsky believed that from birth onward, the "individual constructs the idea of his own

person in the likeness of another individual, receiving his speech reflexes, and thus 'settling' the other in his own organism." (Yaroshevsky, cited in Wink & Putney, 2003, p. xxi)

- **Internal**. Vygotsky broke from the behaviorists and the school of developmental psychology which was at that time led by Jean Piaget who held that development begins internally and individually. Vygotsky believed the opposite is true with his view that learning begins on what he calls an "interpersonal plane" through interaction with others, then moves to what he called an "intrapersonal plane," as concepts are internalized by the individual. "The transformation of an interpersonal process into an intrapersonal one is the result of a long series of developmental events" (Vygotsky, 1978, p. 57)

- **Innatist**. Vygotsky departed from the prevailing view of biological determinism that placed entirely too much emphasis of the role of genetics in human development. In taking this position he was challenging the very foundations of the rising tide of "racial purity" policies in America and Europe. Wink and Putney describe Vygotsky's challenge to this aspect of reductionist thinking.

> In other words, mental functions are socially, culturally, and historically constructed rather than genetically determined. According to Wertsch (1991), Vygotsky's *general genetic law of cultural development* claims that an individual's mental functioning derives from participating in social life, and that what occurs in internalization is not a mere copying of socially organized processes, but transformations of processes at an individual level. (Note: the term *genetic* in this case has nothing to do with inheritance or innateness; rather it refers to *genesis* or origins). (Wink & Putney, 2003, pp. xxi–xxii)

However this does not mean that Vygotsky completely ruled out the effects of genetics. The problem as he viewed was in making the nature versus nurture an "either or" instead of a holistic process. Instead he believed that both aspects form a "unity and struggle of the opposites intertwined in the same process."(Vygotsky, 1993, p. 283) Earlier in the same essay he wrote that:

> Development is not a simple function which can be wholly determined by adding X units of heredity to Y units of environment. It is a historical complex which, at every stage, reveals the past which is part of it. In other words the artificial duality of environment and heredity can misdirect us for it leads us away from the fact that development is a continuous and self-conditioning process, rather than a puppet which can be managed by jerking two strings. (ibid., p. 282)

In sum, Vygotsky's work took on a quest for a new psychology that might be able to bring synthesis to the opposing positions of behaviorism and theories of consciousness. He stated this simply in his famous speech in 1924. "Mind (*psichika*) without behavior does not exist, but behavior without mind does not exist either, because they are one" (quoted in Kozulin, 1990, p. 74).

Lev Vygotsky was 28 years old when he moved to Moscow and every year after that was like living on borrowed time. By 1924 he only had ten more years to live and during much of this time, he would struggle with completely debilitating bouts of consumption while continuing to work up to sixteen-hour days. His daughter shared in an interview that "In 1925 and '26, the outbreak of the disease was so severe that doctors measured his remaining life in terms of 2–3 months. He realized that the end was close. While lying still in the hospital he furiously started to write his famous work entitled *Historical Meaning of the Crisis in Psychology.* (Vygodskaya in Lowe, 2009)

Somehow, doctors managed to save Lev Semyno-vich using a special medical procedure that they had to repeat every month. In 1925, his daughter Gita was born and his other daughter, Asha, was born in 1930. Alexander Romanovich was responsible for distributing free permits to sanatoriums. He got the best permit for Vygotsky, but when he brought it to his friend, Vygotsky tore the permit to pieces. He didn't want to survive at the possible harm coming to Luria (*his co-worker: italics mine*) for providing the permit. (Lowe, 2009)

Creative Collaboration

Shortly after moving to Moscow, Vygotsky formed a research group with two men with similar interests in the creation of a new Soviet psychology that "would focus its attention on uniquely human higher mental processes." This small band of three would become famously known as the *Troika*, from the Russian word for a group of three. Little did they know at the time that their work would have a universal impact on views of human development and learning, especially in the field of educational psychology from their humble beginning up to the present. Alexander Luria would outlive Vygotsky by 43 years and would advance and establish the work of the Troika in **neuropsychology**. In the time after Vygotsky's death, Luria's life work would make a significant impact on a young American researcher named Michael Cole, who would in turn become instrumental in advancing the work of the Troika in the United States. Aleksei Leontiev would outlive Vygotsky by 45 years and would become known as the leading scholar in the theory of activity in the development of higher forms of consciousness. This concept was derived from Marx by Vygotsky but Leontiev would become the primary advocate for it after Vygotsky's death and through Michael Cole and others would inspire a new generation of researchers in the late 20th and early 21st century

Neuropsychology

A branch of psychology that studies the neural connections that exist between the brain and behavior.

such as James Wertsch, Vera John-Steiner, Barbara Rogoff, Yrjo Engestrom, Luis Moll, Lois Holzman, Dot Robbins and many others from all over the planet. (Kozulin, 1990, p. 110)

These three met once or twice a week to develop their research agenda, which always sought to deal with social problems in the lives of the marginalized victims of the crossfire of the ongoing civil war in Russia at the time. They also helped to establish psychological services for secondary schools and, according to Kozulin, the Troika members were involved in a wide range of activities including lecturing and conducting research for only symbolic pay. (1990)

> Luria was the head of the psychological laboratory at the Academy of Communist Education, while Vygotsky had already made the first steps toward the establishment of a center for the study of handicapped children by 1925. The troika soon attracted new members and thus became a "magnificent eight", including Lidia Bozhovich, Roza Levina, Natalya Morozova, Liya Slavina and Alexander Zaporozhets. The work of the group was truly collective. All of the members accepted Vygotsky's theoretical leadership and each was free to use Vygotsky's ideas in his or her own research. (Kozulin, 1990, p. 111)

All of these participants went on to have meaningful and productive careers in this newly formed branch of psychology while demonstrating what would become central to Vygotsky's theories about the socialized aspects of learning and the power of collaboration in the zone of proximal development, which Vygotsky replicated in all of his work, not as a theory but as a constant reality in his practice. His daughter Gita quotes Elkonin, a student of Vygotsky as an example of the kind of team player he actually was.

> Lev Semonovich possessed an extraordinary ability to give support. I have probably never met a single

person who was so little interested in proclaiming his own authorship as Lev Semonovich. It was the extraordinary generosity and scope of ideas of the kind of person who gave everything to everyone. (Vygodskaya, 1999, p. 37)

Vygotsky on Development and Regression

Vygotsky's quest for understanding human development and consciousness was focused on bringing practical social change in the lives of those who had been labeled abnormal. In 1924 he wrote a paper called "Defect and Compensation" and this marked the beginning of the final phase of his life work during his last ten years. Kozulin reports that Vygotsky's last lecture in 1934 was on clinical neuropsychology. "The psychology of handicapped children, together with the neuro- and psychopathology of adults, were seen by Vygotsky as an indispensible aspect of the general theory of human development." It should be noted here that the term *defectology* was actually more evolved that the word *abnormal*, although now we would refer to those with physical, mental or emotional regression as "special needs" or students in special education. (Vygodskaya, 1999, p. 37; Kozulin, 1990, p. 195)

As he began this work, Vygotsky did not have to look very far for people to help. The Russian Revolution, the First World War and the Russian Civil War of the 1920s left thousands of children wandering the streets of the cities with no home or food. "These were children who had suffered abandonment and deprivation for a period of four to five years and whose development was consequently often severely disturbed." (Kozulin, 1990, p. 196.)

Langford reports that Vygotsky "proved to have an unusual gift for the diagnosis of clinical cases and those with an interest would often come to Moscow to see him make diagnoses." As a result of these successes and his dynamic ability as a lec-

turer, he became very popular with the people. "When he went on a trip, his students were so enthusiastic that some even wrote poems in honour of his travels." (Langford, 2005, p. 14; Kozulin, 1990, p. 195)

From 1925 until his death, Vygotsky worked on organizing and leading research in the Laboratory of Psychology for Abnormal Childhood in Moscow. (The name was changed in 1929 to the Institute of Defectology of the Academy of Pedagogical Sciences and is still in existence today.) This work strengthened his ideas of transcending the popular method of that time of stimulating sensory motor apparatus in the impaired area. "That is why argued Vygotsky, there is not much sense in the attempts to compensate for lost sight by training, for example, the physical acuteness of hearing." Vygotsky's method would be to cultivate higher forms of thinking by means of culturally mediated tools. An excellent example of this would be the use of Braille as a tool to master language input and acquisition that could then in turn, through imagination and conceptual blending, open up much higher expression of personal voice and agency than merely relying on the biological mechanism that heightens sound sensitivity for the blind. (Kozulin, 1990, p. 200)

In the summer of 1925 Vygotsky went as the Russian delegate to the International Congress on the Teaching of Deaf Mutes, held in England. On his way home, he stopped in Germany, France and Holland to visit sites of similar work with students of special education. When he returned home he was struck down by another major bout with tuberculosis and was ordered by doctors to stay in bed. While he was recovering he finished his doctoral dissertation titled *The Psychology of Art*. In the introduction he wrote, "My intellect has been shaped under the sign of Spinoza's words, and it has tried not to be astounded, not to laugh, not to cry, but to understand." (Vygotsky cited in Blanck, 1990, p. 41)

After Vygotsky recovered his health enough to travel in 1929, he was a guest lecturer for a short time in Tashkent, in what is now part of Uzbekistan. His students were teachers and psychologists at the First Central Asian State University. While he was there he wrote a stunning letter to the five students who joined the Troika and became the *Eight*. It is worth citing this primary source completely here.

My dear friends,

You are beginning to realise the enormity of the task facing the psychologist attempting to restore the history of the human psyche. You are entering unexplored territory.

When I noticed that in you earlier, I reacted with surprise. And to this day, I find it amazing that in the face of the given circumstances and remaining uncertainties, people who are only just beginning have chosen such a path. I was quite surprised when Alexander Romanovich Luria was the first to take that path in his time, and when Alexei Nikolayevich Leontiev followed in his footsteps. And I am overjoyed to see that I am no longer alone in my quest and that there are not just the three of us: there are five more brave souls setting out on this particular road to knowledge.

A sense of the enormity of the tasks facing contemporary psychology (we are living in an epoch of cataclysm in this field) is my most basic feeling. And that places an infinite responsibility—a most serious, almost tragic (in the finest, most genuine sense of the word) burden on the shoulders of those few who are conducting research in any new branch of science—and especially the science of the person. You must test yourself a thousand times and endure countless ordeals before you make a decision, because this torturous path demands total devotion of self...

Yours,
L. Vygotsky.
Tashkent, 15 April 1929.
(Vygotsky, 1982b, p. 158)

Vygotsky's Final Years

Vygotsky continued at a full-throttle pace in the next two years of his life as a researcher-teacher and prolific writer. During this time he wrote nearly 50 articles. His lifetime interest in the psychology of art and creativity surfaced again from 1930 until the end of his life. We will discuss his views on creativity more fully in chapter four.

Another interesting aspect of Vygotsky's work during this time was his lectures on drama and acting at the Chamber Theater of Moscow. The fact that he engaged in this work even in his weakened physical condition, all the while knowing that his life would be cut short, reveals so much about the value he placed on the role of the arts in creating higher levels of consciousness, both socially and individually. For example in this period, he "co-directed with Luria, film director Eisenstein, and linguist Nicholai Marr a seminar in the field of art, which was considered outstanding." He met frequently with Eisenstein to discuss how the abstract ideas of historical materialism could be depicted in movie images. (Blanck, 1990, p. 41–42; Vygodskaya, 1984)

Vygotsky's passion for researching the influence of cultural-historical factors in shaping consciousness drew his team of scholars to a cross-cultural inquiry in Uzbekistan in 1931 and 1932. He was not able to travel himself at this time, so Luria led a team of people including a German named Kurt Koffka, one of the pioneers in Gestalt psychology.

He continued his fevered pitch of life right up to the end and published three major works during that time. *Adolescent Pedagogy* (1931), *Play and Its Role in the Mental Development of the Child* (1933) and *Thinking and Speaking* (1934). In his last days "Vygotsky acquired the habit of dictating his ideas to a stenographer, who would return them, typed a couple of days later. From his deathbed, he dictated the last chapter of *Thinking and Speech.*" This last book is by far Vygotsky's most popular work, and we will de-

vote all of chapter three of this book to the ideas contained in it. His daughter describes his tragic and last days in Lowe's (2009) documentary. (Blanck, 1990, p. 42).

> Gita Vygodskaya: He knew that the end was close and he tried to accomplish what he wished to do and to deliver the ideas which came into his head. Moreover, I remember quite well when, in the spring of 1934, not long before the end, an unusual conversation between my father and mother took place. They had never talked about the subject in front of me, but it happened that I witnessed their discussion. Mother was saying that doctors insisted on hospitalization and asked him to stop working. Father refused quite flatly. He was a very soft-spoken man. "There is no point to ruin the students' term," he said. "As soon as I finish the academic year we will arrange my stay in the hospital." This conversation took place in March, but on the 9th of May, he was brought home from work suffering a throat hemorrhage. I remember the exact day. It was my birthday and I had a group of children at home. In the morning, my father told me before going to work, "I will try to come home earlier." And after they brought father home from work, he asked me to come closer and said very softly, "I have promised you I would come, so here I am."

Those were the last words he said to his daughter before he died at the age 37 of a throat hemorrhage in the middle of the night between June 10 and 11, 1934. He was buried in Novodevichy Cemetery in Moscow. Dobkin, his childhood friend, recounts Vygotsky's last words. "Vygotsky was fond of ambiguous words and expressions and riddles which lent themselves to different interpretations. When he realised that he was dying, his last words were: 'I'm ready. . . .' This too, could be interpreted in a number of ways." (Dobkin quoted in Levitin, 1982, p. 20)

Books and Manuscripts Banned by the Bolsheviks

On July 4, 1936, two years after Vygotsky's death, the decree of the Communist Party's central committee called for a complete "purge" of all of Vygotsky's work. In addition to the physical removal of his books and manuscripts, his daughter reported:

> There were disgusting articles and books in which he was depicted as an idiot or a threat to society. Consequently, his books were confiscated. Even in the central public library, his articles were cut out and destroyed. Instead of the missing pages, there was a special stamp that said, "Cut out according to the decree of the central committee dated July 4th 1936." (Vygodskaya in Lowe, 2009)

Contemporary Vygotsky scholar Tamara Lifanova shares an example of the thoroughness of the purge of Vygotsky's work.

> It took three months for me to be able to get permission to view a book written by Freud, "Beyond the Pleasure Principle." What I was looking for was the introduction written by Vygotsky. You can imagine my surprise when although you could read Freud's book in Russian, there was no introduction written by Vygotsky. And again, the same stamp, it was removed because it was pedagogical material. (Lifanova in Lowe, 2009)

Of course the "Great Purges" as they came to be known were not limited to official censorship of written material. Thousands of intellectuals were killed or sent to the labor camps and many Vygotsky scholars, including James Wertsch, believe that if Vygotsky had lived longer, he would have also been sent to his death in Siberia. "The really terrible years were in 1936 and '37 (when) the Great Purges were just getting underway. I think there's little doubt, at all, that Vygotsky would have disappeared one way

or the other, been executed, died in camps, or whatever." (Wertsch, in Lowe, 2009)

For someone as committed to the ideas of Karl Marx "not as an icon, but as a real thinker belonging to the European cultural tradition," it is fascinating that Vygotsky's work should be banned for not being sufficiently Marxist-Leninist because of the connections to "bourgeois philosophy" and Western ideas. Yet in the intense climate of fear of reprisal and threat, many rival students of psychology claimed that their methods represented a true version of Marxism while accusing other groups, like Vygotsky's circle, of being too theoretical because his work defied easy categorization. (Kozulin, 1990, p. 242)

The crisis finally came to a head when the Central Committee of the Communist Party took an official stand against **"pedology"** in 1936, which led to the removal of "all those works in educational psychology which transcended traditional pedagogy, (which) covered much of what Vygotsky had studied in the 1920's." In addition to this, "almost all learning disabled children were removed from special classes to ordinary ones" in an attempt to create an orthodoxy that ended methods that defied central control. (Kozulin, 1990, pp. 242–243)

Pedology
is distinct from pedagogy, which refers to the art and science of teaching. Pedology at that time was more the domain of the mental and physical development aspect of children as measured through psychological tests and medical examinations.

The Preservation and Dissemination of Vygotsky's Work

During Stalin's great purges the fate of Vygotsky's manuscripts and intellectual heritage was in the care of his closest friends and family members. The dramatic story of how they were preserved is best conveyed to us through Valerie Lowe's interviews in her 2009 video. His daughter relates the first section followed by Tamara Lifanova, then James Wertsch in the third section.

Gita: Most of his close friends, associates, and colleagues worked there (at the Moscow Institute)

and from there he conducted his research until the end. It was from this institute his coffin was carried to the cemetery. And there was an associate who appeared to be employed as an agent with the People's Commissariat of Internal Affairs. This agent was searching for Vygotsky's books at the institute and making sure that everybody burned them.

Tamara: Many people hid Vygotsky's books under their clothes and under their coats when agents, probably KGB agents, went searching their apartments. Only thanks to this were six volumes of Vygotsky's works saved in different private and state archives so they could be printed. I worked at Alexander Luria's place, at his archives, and also in the archives of other specialists. Many of Lev Semonovich's works were destroyed, actually, the majority of them. Luria told me that several of Lev's works had been translated into English. The Russian versions were destroyed and survived only as English versions. Later, it was a very difficult task to publish them because his works had to be translated from English, back into Russian, a double translation. The works in their English versions did not really allow researchers to know the true, original meaning of his phrases.

James: When Stalin died in 1953, to me, one of the most intriguing chapters in all this is: In 1956, the first volume of Vygotsky's works comes out under the leadership of people like Luria and Leontiev. So as his students, even though they might have disagreed, even though there might have been competition for "what's the real theory," "mine," or whatever, they were instrumental in creating a Vygotskian or neo-Vygotskian school of thought in Moscow in those years.

From 1936 until the early 1960s not much was known about Vygotsky's work in his own country or anywhere else and certainly not in the Western world where the prevailing worldviews prioritized

individual development and achievement through the lens of behaviorism.

One of the early connections to Vygotsky's work came through Jerome Bruner. When I wrote to him to ask him about his initial connection to Vygotsky's work, he replied with this:

> As I recall, my introduction to Vygotsky came when Eugenia Hanfmann was working on a translation of what was to be Vygotsky's first book in English, *Thought and Language* published in 1962 by MIT Press. You'll recall that I wrote an Introduction to that book. I had earlier become acquainted with Vygotsky's work through Alexander Romanovich Luria who was the Professor of Psychology at Moscow with whom I visited in Moscow on several occasions. He was a great admirer of Vygotsky and his work and felt strongly that my own work on perception and cognition generally were very much in the Vygotskian mode. For my part, I felt in those days that Vygotsky was an important corrective to the Piagetian culturally-blind approach to child development. I think that it was that aspect of my own work that led to my being asked to write an introduction to the Vygotsky volume. (Bruner, personal communication, October 2, 2010)

It is historically intriguing to consider that even though Vygotsky's most popular book to date is *Thought and Language* for which Bruner wrote the introduction, the book was still only read initially by a relatively small group of scholars and graduate students. It was only after the turbulent 1960s and 1970s cultural revolution in the United States when alternatives to individualism and behaviorism were sought out to address issues of marginalized students that Vygotsky's work began to be in demand.

One of the key people that were instrumental in helping to advance this work is Michael Cole. In 1962 he and his wife went to Moscow as post-doctoral fellows to study with Luria. During this

time, Luria sought to persuade Cole to translate some of Vygotsky's work into English. Cole was reluctant at first, but after more than a decade back in the United States, Cole along with Vera John-Steiner, Sylvia Scribner and Ellen Souberman began translating the manuscripts that became the second English-language volume of Vygotsky's writings, *Mind in Society.* In the epilogue to Luria's autobiography, Cole relates how his own thinking changed as a result of this editorial project.

> In struggling to understand Vygotsky well enough to resolve our editorial group's different interpretations of his ideas, I slowly began to discern the enormous scope of his thinking. His goal had been no less than the total restructuring of psychological research and theory. This undertaking would never have occurred to me or, I suspect, to very many other psychologists of my generation as anything but a crackpot scheme. Yet Vygotsky was no crackpot, and his scheme was extremely interesting. (Cole & Cole, 1979, Epilogue)

From 1978 to the present, Vygotsky's insights into pedagogy and development have become more and more popular, especially with students and teachers of early childhood education and practitioners of language instruction. In the present climate of the 21st century, there is an increasing demand to understand and develop Vygotsky's ideas of social processes of learning, development and the role of mediation in the creation of higher order thinking, consciousness and creativity. Newman and Holtzman offered this insight into Vygotsky studies from 1978 to 1988.

> The decade 1978–88 was a period of intense research activity. The group of psychologists, linguists, anthropologists and educators working and training others in the Vygotskian tradition grew and became international, to the point where in the late 1980s the existence of a Vygotsky "revival"

was noted (Holzman, 1989; Kozulin, 1986a). In the Soviet Union and many other countries, there was an upsurge in the publication of Vygotsky's writings (suppressed in the Soviet Union for fifty years) and works about Vygotsky and Vygotskian research—in 1988–91 alone, no fewer than seven new books appeared. Increasingly, we find references to Vygotsky's relevance to practitioners in early childhood, special education and adult literacy in newsletters and publications of associations for professionals and paraprofessionals in these fields, such as the American Montessori Society and the American Federation of Teachers. Textbooks in developmental psychology that formerly had devoted a couple of sentences (at most) to Vygotsky now treat him as a "school" nearly on a par with Piaget, Freud, Skinner and social learning theorists, and the recently established US National Teacher Examination includes questions on Vygotsky. To all intents and purposes Lev Vygotsky, the radical Marxist psychologist, has entered the mainstream of psychology. (1993, pp. 8–9)

Why Vygotsky Now?

According to the Google Labs ngram Viewer which tracks the number of times a word appears in published form, there has been a 1,000% increase in references to Vygotsky since the late 1980s (Retrieved February 13, 2011, from http://ngrams.googlelabs. com/graph?content=vygotsky&year_start=1800& year_end=2010&corpus=0&smoothing=3)

This period roughly coincides with the rise of standardized testing brought on by the implementation of the business model in education that gained momentum during the Reagan presidency during the drive for excellence in education. The next manifestation of this trend came about during the Clinton administration's push for a national curriculum starting in 1994 with the initiation of

Goals 2000, followed by the No Child Left Behind Act of 2003, and finally the policy of the Obama administration's Race to the Top. In spite of all the time, energy and literally billions of dollars spent on textbooks and test preparation materials, not to mention the corresponding emotional and even physical trauma experienced by teachers and students alike, tests scores have remained about the same. Here is an example of test scores for 12th graders from 1992–2009 taken from the National Center for Education Statistics website.

> Highlights of the national results in 2009 show that the overall average reading score for twelfth-graders was 2 points higher than in 2005, but 4 points lower than in 1992. There were no significant changes from 1992 to 2009 in the reading score gaps between White and Black students or between White and Hispanic students. (Retrieved March 13, 2011 from: http://nces.ed.gov/pubsearch/pubsinfo.asp?pubid=2011455)

In contrast to these startling conditions, there are a growing number of educators and researchers that are well aware of the value of Vygotskian approaches to the co-construction of knowledge and the dynamic potential of learning within sociocultural contexts and zones of proximal development. There are many areas of Vygotsky's later work that focus on the power of emotion, the use of drama and the arts and creativity in learning that have been frequently ignored in the present climate of standardized curricular practices. In the next two chapters we will discuss two of Vygotsky's most popular ideas, the zone of proximal development, followed by notion of the dialectical relationship between thinking and speech. In the last chapter we will explore some aspects of his "unfinished" work from the last months of his life. These themes include the role of imagination, creativity and the emotions in creating higher levels of consciousness.

Glossary

Consciousness—self-awareness including the capacity to think, feel, form concepts, reflect on one's own thinking as well as creatively and critically imagine.

Dialectical historical materialism—Marx's notion that "a system of matter in motion may, as a result of the conflict of tendencies within itself develop new laws that were not there from the start." (Langford, 2005, p. 23) These new laws create changes in societies that shape the way people think. Marx states that it is "not the consciousness of men that determines their being, but, on the contrary, their social being that determines their consciousness." This can be illustrated from biology through the notion that a goldfish grows in direct proportion to the size of the body of water in which it is placed. However it is important to remember that from both Marx and Vygotsky's viewpoints, that it is the social dimension of influence that is central and not just an individual fish in a pond. (1997, n.p.).

Erudite—Showing depth and breadth of learning and scholarship.

Mechanical materialism—a static view of history that is void of the concept of development. In this view all matter is comprised of a system of mechanical bodies that "existed at the start of time and will exist at the end of time. The laws of motion and the way forces interact always remain the same." (Langford, 2005, p. 23)

Neuropsychology—a branch of psychology that studies the neural connections that exist between the brain and behavior.

Pale of Settlement—This was the allotted land in Czarist Russia where Jews were allowed to live.

Pedology—is distinct from pedagogy which refers to the art and science of teaching. In Vygotsky's lifetime pedology was centered in the domain of the mental and physical development aspect of children as measured through psychological tests and medical examinations.

Personal agency—This refers to the personal ability to take charge of one's own learning, life and unique circumstances.

Pogrom—a Russian word that literally means "destruction," which took on the meaning of an organized mass attack against a community of Jews that was either directly or indirectly officially sanctioned.

In and out of the Zone of Proximal Development

Development, according to a well-known definition, is precisely the struggle of opposites (Vygotsky, 1993, p. 283).

What children can do with the assistance of others is even more indicative of their mental development than what they can do alone (Vygotsky, 1978, p. 85).

Zone of Proximal Development

The developmental space between a learner's actual and potential levels of thinking, problem solving, acting and being.

Any of the scholars and teachers that are familiar with Vygotsky would agree that the most widely known concept that is connected with Vygotsky's work is the **Zone of Proximal Development**. In fact, students of educational psychology from all over the world are at least familiar with some of the ideas connected to it. But there are also many misappropriations of this concept. For example the zone of proximal development necessitates the "assistance of others" in a social context of learning as the

above quote mentions. In Vygotsky's view this involves another person who is more advanced in the target learning domain that can negotiate the point of learning in a way that leads to development. This is impossible as an independent activity that is withdrawn from consistent human interaction.

Another misconception is seen in thinking that a simple rearrangement of classroom furniture will create a zone of proximal development (ZPD). There are at least two errors in this approach. First, the ZPD is not a geographical zone but refers rather to the "space" between the learner's actual level of experience and their potential level of development. Second, Vygotsky is very clear on the role of the mentor-teacher to lead in development even though the goal is the co-construction of knowledge. In this context it becomes necessary to distinguish between a "student centered" approach and a "learner centered" one. In both approaches, what the student is able to internalize is more important than a "top down" method which is characterized by a teacher-centered delivery of instruction. But in a learner-centered environment, the teacher or mentor is able to maintain certain parameters within the target subject matter in an environment of interaction and dialogue that enhances student voice and personal agency. (Trent Maurer, personal communication August 15, 2010)

There are many similarities between Vygotsky's view of learner centeredness and problem-solving/problem-posing education and that of the Brazilian educator Paulo Freire (1921–1997), and although they obviously never knew each other they were both influenced similarly by Hegel and Marx. Joe Kincheloe had this to say about Freire's approach to teaching. The parallels to Vygotsky's views are striking.

By promoting problem posing and student research, teachers do not simply relinquish their authority in the classroom. Over the last couple of decades several teachers and students have misunderstood the subtlety of the nature of teacher authority in a critical pedagogy. Freire in the last years of his life was very concerned with this issue and its misinterpretation by those operating in his name. Teachers, he told me, cannot deny their position of authority in such a classroom. It is the teacher, not the students, who evaluates student work, who is responsible for the health, safety, and learning of students. To deny the role of authority the teacher occupies is insincere at best, dishonest at worst. Critical teachers, therefore, must admit that they are in a position of authority and then demonstrate that authority [sic] in their actions in support of students. One of the actions involves the ability to conduct research/produce knowledge. The authority of the critical teacher is **dialectical**; as teachers relinquish the authority of truth providers, they assume the mature authority of facilitators of student inquiry and problem posing. In relation to such teacher authority, students gain their freedom—they gain the ability to become self-directed human beings capable of producing their own knowledge. (Kincheloe, 2008, p. 17)

This notion of the role of the teacher in the ZPD brings us to Vygotsky's use of the Russian word for education, **obuchenie,** which is translated as teaching but "is interchangeable for the activity of the teachers and students." This means that Vygotsky viewed teaching as learning and therefore confirms what we said about the role of teachers in the progressive classroom. In the mind of Vygotsky, the zone of proximal development is an environment out of which the teacher and the student co-construct and create knowledge together rather than just moving in the "top down" approach that Freire calls the "banking model" of education wherein the teacher makes "deposits" of knowledge into the empty "account" of the student and draws the information back out on test days in the exact form and manner in which it was deposited. (Wink & Putney, 2003, p. xxiii)

Obuchenie

The Russian word for education, that unlike the English word which separates the function of teaching and learning, instead means that there is a mutual dependence and intertwining of teacher and learner in one holistic process.

Contrasting Views of Learning and Development

In this chapter, we will use the dialectical method discussed in Chapter One to explore more fully what the zone of proximal development is and is not. Vygotsky was a genius at being able to holistically explore opposing viewpoints and paradoxical ideas and there is much to be gained from looking at his work in a similar way.

Vygotsky's studies in psychology were all predicated on his desire to establish a clear understanding of the dialectical relationship between learning and development beyond the prevailing views of the time. In Chapter Six of Vygotsky's *Mind in Society* he outlines three major theoretical positions of learning and development before sharing his own view of the ZPD. Even though this was originally written more than ninety years ago, it is remarkable on one hand to observe how little has changed from his day to the current time, and on the other hand, to view Vygotsky's concepts as forward thinking and relevant to present conditions in education. In *Mind in Society*, Vygotsky's presentation of contrasting views starts with Piaget's theory that development precedes learning, followed by the behaviorist theory that learning and development occur simultaneously as nothing more than conditioned reflexes. Third, he addresses Kurt Koffka's (a German contemporary) attempt to split the difference between Piaget's views and **behaviorism** but in the process, "fails to resolve the issue but confuses it" by misinterpreting both extreme positions. Let us look more closely at the error in these three perspectives before focusing on a summary of Vygotsky's views of development. (Vygotsky, 1978, pp. 79–91; Vygotsky, 1987d, p. 197)

Behaviorism

A school of psychology that is focused on measurable and observable behaviors in subjects that are motivated by external stimuli and operant conditioning. In educational contexts, behaviorism views learning as a set of habits acquired in individualized and measured with standardized methods of testing.

Development Preceding Learning

It should be mentioned from the outset that during Vygotsky's tenure as a researcher, views of intelligence as a product of genetics were becoming in-

creasingly popular in the West and rose to prominence in Nazi Germany. Henry Goddard's ideas acted as a catalyst for the creation of I.Q. tests and federally enacted policies of **eugenics**. Goddard's view of biological intelligence left very little to environmental influences. For example, he claimed that "the mental level for each individual is determined by the kind of chromosomes that come together with the union of the germ cells: that it is but little affected by any later influences except serious accidents as may destroy part of the mechanism." In sharp contrast to this, Vygotsky's view of the internalization process of knowing gives centrality to cultural and social influences in learning and development and shuns a fixed or static measure of intelligence derived exclusively from biology. (1920, p. 1)

With the inclusion of Goddard's position, all of these views come under the general heading of behaviorism with its emphasis on learning as a set of habits, accomplished through memorization of material that is often removed from the context of real life. The learning by habit methodology focuses uses drills and repetition through stimulus and response, and is situated in an individualistic approach to schooling that is contained within a broad context of biological rather than socio-historical processes. We will discuss this in more detail below.

Jean Piaget's view that development must precede learning is also genetically based even though his theories are more finely nuanced than classical behaviorism. Vygotsky respected Piaget's work in many ways but ultimately moved beyond it in favor of a much more fluid concept of learning and development. The following imaginary dialogue from an education class developed by Chris Kerfoot describes the problem with this approach in contrast to Vygotsky's views. (Used with permission from Wink & Putney, 2003, pp. 25–28)

How did Piaget and Vygotsky come to view learning and development? How did their views differ? Why does it matter to us?

Eugenics
is a word that was created by Francis Galton to refer to the science of human reproduction that has as its goal the "improvement" of the human species through selective breeding and population control.

One of the significant differences in theory between Piaget and Vygotsky is that: Piaget believed that development preceded learning, whereas Vygotsky believed that learning precedes development. For Piaget, a student could not learn something until she was developmentally ready. However, Vygotsky believed that learning pulled development to higher levels. This difference has the potential for profound impact on teaching and learning today. We offer the following vignette to demonstrate how this theoretical difference might look in classrooms.

Jean and Pia are student teachers in first-grade classrooms. Dr. V is their university supervisor. Dr. V was once a first-grade teacher, and her teaching is grounded in Vygotsky's socio-historical theory. Dr. V arranged for both student teachers to meet together throughout the semester with her so that they could learn from discussing their experiences with different mentor teachers and in different classrooms. Dr. V knew that both student teachers came from a Piagetian background and had not yet had the opportunity to study Vygotsky. Therefore, her goal was to share a Vygotskian perspective on learning and development with them. Dr. V hoped that their learning would enhance their own development.

DR. V: Jean and Pia, you've both had one week of student teaching. How is it going so far?

PIA: I'm trying to discover where my students are developmentally and then go from there. They need experiences with the real world and using things they are familiar with to demonstrate the concepts of addition and subtraction.

DR. V: It also helps to talk through what you are doing. The students will use the language they hear from you to internalize the concepts. In other words, it will get them thinking. Try some predictions and problem solving.

JEAN: I thought that requiring first graders to think about two things at once is beyond

their ability. They're not yet at the stage where they can do it. It's just going to take them more time.

DR. V: Talk with the students about what you as a group are doing. Ask questions along the way. Have the students do an activity in pairs so they can talk with each other.

JEAN: I'm doing some graphing activities, and I started with real objects.

DR. V: This is good, you are both thinking about what you can do to make your lessons meaningful. Don't forget that speaking and thinking go together, and if you get the kids talking about what they are doing, they'll take it in and understand it better. How is reading going?

PIA: I can't seem to get the low readers interested in reading. During silent reading time I have to force them to read. Most of them sit and stare at their books or just talk to each other.

JEAN: Silent reading doesn't work too well with first graders; developmentally, are they ready for it?

DR. V: What would happen if you encouraged the students to read aloud so they can hear what they are reading, and try partner reading?

PIA: Make sure the books they have to read are on their level.

JEAN: Yes, but I found some children's magazines about animals that they like to talk about. I know these magazines are too difficult for them to read so I wasn't going to use them for reading class. But Kwan keeps going to those magazines. Yesterday he sat next to Beto, and they both looked at those magazines together. They kept whispering about those animals, and I was wondering if I should send them to the time-out center.

DR. V: What happened when they whispered about the animals? Talking helps them to reflect on what they know and helps them think about things in new ways. Did they

learn from each other through this informal conversation?

Much later in the semester, Dr. V met with Jean and Pia in order to assess their student teaching. First, she needed to listen to them.

DR. V: How is it going with your student teaching?

PIA: I'm beginning to see the importance of observing my students. I learn a lot by watching them. I try to ask myself questions: What can they do on their own? What can they do with a little help?

JEAN: I've also seen how important it is for students to learn by doing. It was hard at first, because I felt like I didn't have control over anything. Eventually, I saw that if I structured classroom materials and situations so that they are in line with my objectives, learning took place and I was able to guide students in the right direction.

PIA: I also found it helpful to ask questions. This encouraged my students to grow in their learning and develop new ideas. Of course, it helped to have them interact with each other, many students are very creative, and I sometimes find myself learning from them.

DR. V: Pia, how is the silent reading going?

PIA: It's going really well, but it's no longer silent. The students seem to enjoy reading more when they are reading aloud and reading to each other.

JEAN: Remember Kwan and Beto? I didn't think they could read those harder magazines, but in science the other day, they were both going on and on about how a baby kangaroo incubates in the mama's pouch for weeks. Did they learn by talking about those pictures?

DR. V: Could be that more was going on there than met the eye. Ok, and the math lessons?

JEAN: I'm seeing how important it is to use concrete examples-especially when I'm introducing something new. It really helps them

understand. Oh, and after explaining something, I have a few students demonstrate to the whole class.

DR. V: Modeling is always important. Having some students model for the others helps them feel that they are an important part of the group.

PIA: I have a few students who always seem to get things right away. I've grouped them with the students who need a little more help. They enjoy being the "teachers." Makes me wonder if the students sometimes learn more from each other than from me.

JEAN: And it takes a lot of time and planning to figure out how to connect concrete experiences to symbolic thinking. Children think differently from adults. What makes perfect sense to me might be totally foreign to my students.

PIA: I'm amazed at what they learn from each other. Learning really is a social experience and I think using language in this way expands their thinking.

DR. V: Hmm, seems like learning leads development. Do you see any connection between your students learning from each other and the meetings we've had together?

JEAN: Well, I hadn't thought of it before now, but I guess we have been learning from each other.

PIA: We've taken ideas from these discussions and used them in our own classrooms.

DR. V: If you think about it, you have been learning in several ways. You have applied what you learned in your courses, and you observed your mentor teachers and conferenced with them about your lessons. Then you talked with me and with each other here in our debriefing sessions. Throughout your student teaching, I have been giving specific directions so you could scaffold your learning. Soon you will be able to teach without my help.

PIA: Having people to talk with has been helpful.

DR. V: Learning for teachers never ends. I agree that talking with others enhances our learning. Our meetings have encouraged me to try new things in my graduate classes. I'll bet you didn't know that I was incorporating some of your ideas into my Classroom Assessment course for teachers, did you?

JEAN: You mean that you learned from us?

DR. V: Of course! We all learned from each other through our collaboration around real-life problems you were having in the classroom. Remember, novices contribute to mentors in their own ways. Good job, both of you!

In the current context of schooling and high stakes testing, the above scenario of a successful change in approaches seems to be the exception rather than the rule. Nevertheless, this kind of reflective practice in the content areas that are addressed seems possible and the nature of the dialogue is in itself an example of the use of mentoring teachers in the "learning preceding development" fashion of Vygotsky.

Views of Learning and Development in Behaviorism

Behaviorism has manifested itself in an array of applications and methods, but at the core is the belief that learning is habit formation developed through connections between stimuli and responses. In this view, learning is development that is formed through the "gradual accumulation of conditioned reflexes." These views were especially prevalent in Soviet Russia during Vygotsky's time under the headings of reflexology and mental measurement. (Newman & Holzman, 1993, p. 58)

Ivan Sechenov and Vladimir Bekhterev were the founders of Russian reflexology. Both believed that "thought is nothing but a reflex" so studies on con-

sciousness and imagination research were not at all considered important. Ivan Pavlov was a follower of these two men with his famous experiments of ringing bells triggering salivation in dogs. The concept of "learning" therefore "is nothing more than the results of the establishment of new nervous connections during the postnatal experience of an organism." Schubert describes this as likening the "mind to muscles that could be developed with practice in subjects of the classical curriculum." Drilling recitation and rote memorization were all means to strengthen the mind. This left little to higher order thinking skills and hands-on contextualized application. This form of isolated learning was especially despised by Vygotsky's contemporary John Dewey. (Kozulin, 1990, p. 74; Pavlov, 1927, p. 26; Schubert, 2002, p. 7). In 1910 Dewey wrote:

> There is a swimming school in a certain city where youth are taught to swim without going into the water, being repeatedly drilled in the various movements which are necessary for swimming. When one of the young men so trained was asked what he did when he got into the water, he laconically replied, [sunk]." (p. 14)

Edward Thorndike's (1913) notion of mental measurement viewed the mind as a machine that could be "oiled" and made more "efficient" in terms of "measurable standardized outcomes." Herbert Kliebard described Thorndike's view of the human mind as "a machine with thousands, indeed millions of individual connections, each containing a message which may have no logical relationship with other messages." This view bolstered the emphasis on "piece rate" production and time management that was strongly emphasized at the height of the machine age in Soviet Russia as well as in the West. In short Thorndike viewed education as "one form of human engineering and will profit by measurement of human nature and

achievement as mechanical and electrical engineering have profited by using the foot-pound, calorie, volt and ampere." (Kliebard, 2004, p. 91; Thorndike, 1921, p. 371)

In response to notions of "mind as machine," Dewey had the following to say, which is very much in keeping with Vygotsky's ideas about higher levels of consciousness, especially the last sentence below.

> Thinking is specific, not a machinelike, ready-made apparatus to be turned indifferently and at will upon all subjects, as a lantern may throw its light as it happens upon horses, streets, gardens, trees, or river. Thinking is specific, in that different things suggest their own appropriate meanings, tell their own unique stories, and in that they do this in very different ways with different persons. As the growth of the body is through the assimilation of food, so the growth of mind is through the logical organization of subject-matter. Thinking is not like a sausage machine which reduces all materials indifferently to one marketable commodity, but is a power of following up and linking. (Dewey, 1910, p. 39)

Koffka's Quest for a Middle Ground

The third view of development addressed by Vygotsky came from the Gestalt school of psychology in general and Koffka's views in particular. He believed that Piaget's idea that development could be isolated from learning and the behaviorist view of learning and development as simultaneous occurrences in response to external stimuli could complement each other through a dualistic view of development. "There is development as maturation and development as instruction." Vygotsky stated that "the interaction is left virtually unexplored in Koffka's work, which is limited solely to general remarks regarding the relation between

these two processes." Nevertheless, Koffka's small shift toward the influences of learning on development opened the door enough to give Vygotsky the direction he needed to move past this duality in the formation of the zone of proximal development. (Newman & Holtzman, 1993, p. 59; Vygotsky, 1978, p. 81)

Vygotsky's View of the Zone of Proximal Development

Any function in the child's cultural development appears twice, or on two planes. First it appears on the social plane, and then on the psychological plane. First it appears between people as an interpsychological category, and then within the child as an intrapsychological category. . . . Social relations or relations among people genetically underlie all higher functions and their relationships. (Vygotsky, 1981, p. 63)

Now we come to some of the general features of the ZPD as they were understood and taught by Vygotsky. Of course these are outlined here below in broad terms since there has been and continues to be so much written about this. (A quick survey using Google yields 1,670,000 total results). We will mention some of the most value points that are relevant to educators.

The zone of proximal development is not focused on a static or fixed level of student achievement. Bodrova and Leong (1996) astutely observed that:

Vygotsky chose the word *zone* because he conceived of development not as a point on a scale, but as a continuum of behaviors or degrees of maturation. By describing the zone as *proximal* (next to, close to), he meant that the zone is limited by those behaviors that will develop in the near fu-

ture. Proximal refers not to all the possible behaviors that will eventually emerge, but to those closest to emergence at any given time. (p. 35)

The current obsession in education with standards-based benchmarks of performance places an undue premium on isolated facts that are regurgitated on standardized tests as the only measure of student achievement. This emphasis has created an entire culture of deficit schooling and thinking and subtractive schooling. Both of these concepts are derived from views of intelligence and performance as biologically based. (Valencia & Solorzano, 1997; Valenzuela, 1999)

In contrast to this, the concept of the ZPD gives centrality to the potential of the student in what Robbins calls height psychology as opposed to a Freudian emphasis on depth psychology, which uses the past to look for the roots or causes of mental and emotional disorders which, again, leads to a deficit view of development. Robbins' take on Vygotskyian psychology, on the other hand, "views the heights of potentiality of the individual, also including unconscious components; and, the unconscious is viewed as the seat of creativity and problem solving. (Robbins, 2011, p. 19)

The following story from Lisa Delpit's (1995) experience provides a good example how the **deficit model of schooling** serves to hide the heights of potential and development in children. This is a story about a first grade African American student named Howard who struggles with the very simplest math work sheets and, as a result, was recommended for special education assessment.

Deficit model of schooling

A view of education that is focused on negative expectations of students derived from stereotypes of ethnicity and socio-economic status or disabilities. The curriculum is often focused on "remediation."

I agreed until I got to know his life outside of school. I discovered that his mom was afflicted with drug problems and that his 3-year old sister had cerebral palsy. Howard got both of them up every morning, dressed his sister, and got both of them on the bus. He had to do a good bit of math

figuring simply to get the right amount of money for the bus. Howard also did the family laundry. He had to keep track of his change for the Laundromat and had to keep from being cheated when he bought detergent. (p. 39)

In this case, Howard was very fortunate to have Lisa Delpit as his teacher because she was able to see his ZPD included his out of school, real-life learning in context and save him from the downward spiral of increasing educational deficit. Delpit continues her astute analysis of decontextualized deficit schooling by imagining what schools would look like if they took it on themselves to teach African American children how to dance.

Rather than have the children learn from one another in real contexts, the school would have each particular dance broken down into 200 mastery-learning units. Kids would have to complete a workbook and pass paper-and-pencil tests on each unit before moving on to learn the first half of the first hand movement of the first dance. By the end of the year, we would have a slew of remedial African-American dancers. (Delpit, 1995, p. 39)

In the next chapter we will discuss some of the ways that language is especially instrumental is connecting unconscious and subconscious processes with creativity and problem solving. But as we continue to discuss the dynamic of potentiality in the ZPD, the introduction of another term may help to further elucidate Vygotsky's views that Michael Cole (1996) calls **prolepsis**. We introduce this term with a quote from Vygotsky himself.

Prolepsis

The perception of an anticipated or future condition of development before it actually exists as an internalized state of being.

The zone of proximal development defines those functions that have not yet matured but are in the process of maturation, functions that will mature tomorrow but are currently in an embryonic state. These functions could be termed the "buds" or

"flowers" of development rather than the "fruits" of development." (Vygotsky, 1978, p. 86)

Let's use what was probably your experience as an example of this. At some point in your life you were probably told that you had real potential as a teacher or as a graduate student. These predictions are clear examples of Cole's notion of prolepsis which is predicated on Vygotsky's concept of "buds" or "flowers" of development. Prolepsis is a rare and extremely valuable tool in education if teachers and mentors can use it realistically as a means to help students move into spaces that are truly within their grasp through interaction with those who look at the bud and see the fruit until prolepsis becomes internalized by the student themselves. Boris Meshcheryakov refers to this transition as a process of moving from "heteroprolepsis" to "autoprolepsis." (2007, p. 166)

An example of each would be when a parent hears their child humming on key or reproducing entire tunes in various levels of complexity, they will of course, under normal conditions, encourage their offspring toward some future musical activity by reporting their performance to them with something like "when you were two, you could hum all the notes to that song and I know you will do quite well with piano lessons."

Meshcheryakov goes on to relate an example of autoprolepsis in children's role playing when the child imagines "him or herself in various adults' roles (hunter, mother, teacher, etc.), imitating the elements of cultural forms of behavior." Many future and present teachers, for example, can recall a time when they used to pretend to teach their siblings or maybe even their stuffed animals. But this role-play does not cease as we grow out of childhood. In fact, student teaching is an example of learning proceeding development as we saw in the beginning of this chapter with the all too real scenario acted out by Dr. V. Pia and Jean. We will further discuss the value of creative play and activity in Chapter Four. (Meshcheryakov, 2007, p. 167)

The Role of Scaffolding in the ZPD

Scaffolding refers to the temporary use of instructional support that provides the learner ease of access to the targeted zones of the subject matter until it becomes internalized.

The metaphor of **scaffolding** in connection with the ZPD did not originate with Vygotsky. It was actually coined by Jerome Bruner. When he was asked how he came up with the scaffolding metaphor he said that it was "just one of those labeling intuitions that came out of the blue." Scaffolding is (under normal conditions) the temporary framework used in the construction of physical buildings that enables ease of vertical and horizontal access and safety for the workers as they work on the targeted zones of the structure. (Bruner, personal communication, 10/6/10)

When scaffolding is used as a metaphor for education, the meaning is still very similar. It refers to the temporary use of instructional support that provides the learner ease of access to the targeted zones of the subject matter until it becomes internalized. This can take the form of helping the learner by asking them which letter has two humps, or in a more elaborate example, picture a vehicle that is equipped for driver's training with two steering wheels, two gas pedals and two brake pedals. Although these vehicles are less common in the 21st century than they were a few decades ago, they are still used. The following blurb is taken from a driving school website. This direct quote provides an apt example of educational scaffolding in the ZPD.

All Taggart's training vehicles are equipped with two steering wheels, two brakes and two gas pedals. For over 40 years, we have installed the two steering wheel system for two reasons. First is the safety factor. Because the instructor can take over at any time, our students relax and learn faster. Also, the extra steering wheel is a great teaching tool, because the instructor can demonstrate from his/her side, without stopping the car to change seats. It saves a lot of time. (Retrieved on 6/6/11 from: http://www.taggartsdrivingschool.com/adultindex.htm)

Hopefully the driver's training instructor will avoid the kind of antics that were experienced in one school where the teacher applied the brakes at surprisingly odd and random times apparently out of a desire to maintain psychological as well as physical control. This practice put the learners out of the ZPD and certainly made the scaffolding period longer instead of shorter by creating anxiety for the learners.

However in a normal situation of "hands on" drivers training, the instructor may use all of the features of scaffolding in the ZPD through the "gradual withdrawal of adult control and support as a function of children's increasing mastery of a given task." This process is another way to describe Vygotsky's notion of development as it moves from interpersonal activity to an intrapersonal and internalized reality. However this journey is not necessarily linear or evenly spaced in stages. For example, to borrow again from the driver's training analogy, the student may experience relative ease in learning how to make right turns or pass a car on a four lane highway, but parallel parking lessons may even result in mild collisions resulting in temporary loss of motivation to learn at all. Remember from Chapter One Vygotsky's notion of development is built on Hegel's thesis, antithesis, synthesis theory which Kozulin depicts "not a straight ascending line, but a complex trajectory replete with detours and reversals." (1990, p. 16) (Moll & Greenberg, 1990, p. 139)

It would be difficult to visualize such a trajectory, since each learner's process of internalization is unique. Zebroski contrasts the smooth, incremental and linear trajectory of Piaget's notion of development with a Vygotskian image that "appears as an oscillating, sometimes broken sine wave in which the dips and crests of each developmental zone alternate. The wave widens and heightens across time." (p. 162) He goes on to discuss the cumulative effect of development, in spite of periods of up and down, still within the zone of proximal development. "The model is both progressive and regres-

sive, making a very important place for risk taking and apparent 'failure' and 'backward' development, which nonetheless often foreshadow the reorganization and restructuring of experience and prepare for that developmental leap that follows." (Zebroski, 1994, p. 162)

Another example from the driver's training example comes to mind. The student driver is learning to turn left onto a two lane road. She or he is embarrassed about the time it takes for very distant oncoming traffic to pass first because there are impatient drivers, honking their horns in cars and trucks behind the student driver's car that must wait for the left turn to be completed before they can continue. "Oh no, all those people are waiting for me to turn, I hate this. I will never learn to drive." At this point the teacher takes control with the extra steering wheel and gas pedal and makes the left turn with still plenty of time to spare before the oncoming traffic actually reaches the driver's training car. Afterward the teacher and student reflect on the situation and the student is reassured verbally about what to do next. A week later, the same driving situation comes up and the student executes the turn with much more confidence. The next level of course will be realized when the student can make the turn on their own in a normal car. But before we abandon driver's training as an application of the ZPD, we need to go back even further in Vygotsky's notion of development and include the role of play.

The Role of Play in the Zone of Proximal Development

Vygotsky believed that play was one of the highest forms of development for children. He went so far as to say that "a child's greatest achievements are possible in play." Remember in Chapter One when we mentioned how Vygotsky himself, even as a teenager, along with his friends would pretend that they were historic figures? Even in that brief sum-

mary of his short life you can see that almost all his theories came out of some aspect of his life experience. In another piece on this topic, Vygotsky wrote "play creates a zone of proximal development of the child. In play a child always behaves beyond his average age, above his daily behavior; in play it is as though he were a head taller than himself." (p. 102) Undoubtedly, this statement puts play at the very core of the value of the ZPD, especially the notion of "learning leading development" instead of Piaget's reversal of this statement. Wink and Putney add to this idea by writing that "children at play are in a zone of proximal development. In play, children are acting out real-life situations in which they develop rules that move them beyond their current level." Now we return to our driving example. One of the most common things for children to play is pretend driving. Perhaps when you were little you got behind the wheel of the family car and played with the pedals, or maybe you pretended to be a bus driver while singing the children's song "The Wheels on the Bus." All of these experiences have the potential for significant developmental value. Video games that contain driving sequencing are another form of developmental play. The following story shows how development can occur in one area to the exclusion of other vital areas. (Vygotsky, 1978, p. 102; Wink & Putney, 1978, p. 113)

A nine-year-old Japanese schoolboy who learnt how to drive from playing video games has used his motoring skills to steal the family car and to visit his grandmother. Police were alerted to the young boy's antics by reports from members of the public that a car without a driver was moving down a street in the city of Ogaki in central Japan. When he was stopped by police, the schoolboy told officers: "I learned from playing video games at arcades and watching my father drive." The adventure began when the boy, who has not been named, decided to take the family car from the front of his home, where it was parked with the keys in the ignition, in order to visit his grandmother. But soon after he set off on the 7.5 mile journey he became lost. After 1.8 miles the boy pulled into a convenience store car park in order to ask staff for directions. When members of the public called police to claim that a car was being driven without a driver, officers found the vehicle neatly backed into the convenience store car park.

After being found by the police, the boy reportedly told officers: "I'm sorry. I just wanted to go to my grandmother's house." A police spokesman added: "The boy is interested in driving because of video games. He drove the car out of his adventurous mind." (Retrieved June 9, 2011, from: http://www.telegraph.co.uk/news/worldnews/asia/japan/3414259/Boy-learned-to-drive-from-video-games-before-stealing-family-car.html)

One of the clearest examples of the value of play in the ZPD is found in Gallas' work. She describes how students take on the meaning of text and read it from the "inside out" through a process of role playing leading to identity, discourse acquisition and authoring. By using our example of the student driver, we can place Gallas' notion of reading from the "inside out" as beginning with pretend driving, accompanied by Vygotsky's notion about the use of rules and discourse in play. Pretending to respond to traffic signs is a good example of this.

It is important to differentiate between Gallas' use of the term "inside out" and Vygotsky's notion of internalization which is the goal of learning in the ZPD. When Gallas refers to reading from the inside out, she is talking about involving the mind, body and emotions in expressing an identity through a discourse of appropriate language. This process actually leads to Vygotsky's notion of internalization and means that the learner can now perform the target content area on their own. For example, in the driver's training analogy, reading from the "inside out" would be the play and practice stages of driving. Internalization would be experienced when the stu-

dent masters both the written and applied driver's test and consequently has acquired much more information about driving. They have actually become a driver. (Gallas, 2003, pp. 65–75)

Language Identity

Linguists often speak of the power of the language ego. This phenomenon involves the ability to take on the identity of a speaker of any language or dialect. This not only includes target vocabulary and syntax of a language, it also includes gestures and the learner's perceptions of the attitude of the language. An excellent example of this is seen in Jamie Foxx's Oscar-winning portrayal of Ray Charles in the film *Ray*. Anyone who is even vaguely familiar with Ray Charles as a person and performer could easily recognize the outstanding work Foxx did of portraying the "text" of his life. To prepare for his role in the movie, he actually went to a school for the blind, in order to learn how to read Braille and to immerse himself in the culture of blindness. (Benjamin Hakford, 2004)

In language acquisition, there is an unpredictable point when communication becomes part of the subconscious. Anyone who has studied a foreign language intensely is aware that when you begin to think or dream in that language, you are on your way to fluency. By far, the best method of language learning is in the context of real communication, not in the isolation and recitation of specific points of sentence-level grammatical items. Literacy involves imaginative connections to text, speech inflections, gesturing, and the ability to "read" a person's intent.

Reading From the Inside Out

In the present context of literacy education, the great debate between phonics versus whole language instruction seems to never end. The National

Reading Panel endorses a strong emphasis on phonics, or bottom-up processing. Others continue to emphasize the role of context in top-down processing. On the surface, Gallas' view of inside-out learning presents a view that is outside this dichotomy. In actuality, both these models are implicit in the inside-out approach as well as Vygotsky's general ideas about language learning as internalization in the ZPD, and externalization in communication. We will cover this in greater depth in the next chapter but mention it now as a way of connecting Gallas' work with the role of play in the ZPD. This model describes three stages of language learning. The first is the identity stage, the second is the discourse acquisition stage, and the third stage involves a concept that she calls "authoring." In order to understand how this approach works, it is essential to briefly describe the features and function of each stage and how they all connect to Vygotsky's work. I do not personally like the word "stage" but use it here for accuracy of citations.

Identity Stage

In the identity stage, the learner takes on the prescribed role of the text. For example, when a student is reading a text from science, through the process of identification, he or she can emulate the role of a scientist by adopting the speech and mannerisms of a scientist, thereby "reading" the text from the "inside out." Gallas quotes from Lave and Wenger in this connection. They write that "learning involves the construction of identities." This theory came alive for her as she took her students on a field trip to a science museum. As four of her students stood next to a display of dinosaur bones, they began to pretend they were scientists. They adopted what they perceived to be the speech and appropriate tone of scientists in their role play. (2003, p. 70)

She further supported this position from her own childhood experience. She remembered learn-

ing about using measurements for cooking when she was a child with a toy oven. She sums up this identity stage by saying that "first the child takes on the role of a scientist; second, the student takes on the point of view of the object or text under study." (p. 74) Of course this is not limited to the field of science. It could just as easily be applied to role playing a figure from history like Vygotsky did with his friends, or being a mathematician or chef or a kayak builder. In a similar way, Vygotsky sees this kind of directed play as the bridge between verbal concepts and real-life experience. "All examinations of the essence of play have shown that in play a new relationship is created between the semantic and the visible—that is, between situations in thought and real situations." (Gallas, 2003, p. 74; Vygotsky, 1933/2002, n.p.)

Discourse Acquisition

The next stage that Gallas presents is discourse acquisition. This stage takes identity several steps further. What is involved here is the appropriation of the identity through a "tool kit...of a discourse" a term she borrowed from the prominent Vygotsky scholar, James Wertsch (1991). This consists of the language, tools, text, and forms of inquiry that are discipline specific and using them to master an identity. She succinctly sums up this stage in saying that "the tools and texts of a subject gain their vitality when they are brought into *productive* (italics, hers) contact with a student's experience." This involves mental, emotional and somatic productivity or what Vygotsky and his colleagues called an "activity." (Gallas, 2003, pp. 86–87)

Gallas' view of discourse acquisition is strongly aligned with Vygotsky's use of one of the most prominent directors in the history of theatrical drama, Konstantin Stanislavsky. In fact his work is still used today in drama education. The system that Stanislavsky developed "was based on the emotive

subtext each actor was supposed to convey by linguistic and paralinguistic means." This work "left a lasting impression on Vygotsky, who used Stanislavsky's note for the actors to demonstrate the role of emotive subtext in the decoding of verbal messages." (Kozulin, 1990, p. 28)

This was the experience of Tonya Perry. In a wonderfully well-written narrative style, she discusses her experience of using exploratory drama to enhance the personal connection to the reading of *The Diary of Anne Frank* to a high school class. She observed a marked difference between the ability to recall facts about the text and the student's ability to comprehend it. Through the use of exploratory drama, she was able to increase empathetic comprehension. She focused on the lines in the text that referred to the periods of silence in the attic that Anne Frank's family had to practice. (2005, p. 120)

> Instead of reading the play the next day, I asked the students to enter the room without talking. As they sat, I told them they were all hiding from the Nazi forces like Anne Frank. Immediately, without any additional description, I showed them video clips of what we would face if anyone discovered our whereabouts. We quietly watched images of soldiers looking for the Jewish people in their homes and taking them to ghettos. As time progressed, we watched trains fill with people heading to concentration camps. Images of families separating and deplorable living conditions occurred more frequently. Students silently transitioned to the large taped square in the middle of the floor. I asked them to sit quietly for five minutes without talking and think about what we would face if we or someone else talked, placing our lives in grave danger. (p. 122)

This exercise proved to be effective in increasing comprehension by taking vicarious meaning making to a higher level. Perry summed up the value of this exercise by pointing out that "authentic drama

assignments capture the students' ability to understand complex concepts and use them in multiple contexts." What struck me the most about this classroom experience is that the students read the text with great phonetic facility but still lacked the context that was needed to really feel, see, touch, and understand the story. It took place in a zone of proximal development to transcend walls between 21st-century students in Alabama and the scene inside an attic in Nazi-occupied Amsterdam in 1942! I understand the limitations as well. There is no method to fully convey the sheer terror that this family experienced. At the same time, through use discourse and in this case the accompanying rules of silence along with the emotional subtext of fear, the students were able to look through the cracked door into the lives of others though identifying with the text and "reading it" with their bodies. Before moving to the last phase of play in the ZPD, let's stop to connect some of Vygotsky's terminology to the above learning scenario. (Perry, 2005, p. 122)

Authoring

The final phase of this process Gallas calls "authoring" by a public act of presenting it in another form, for a real audience. This can be accomplished through a musical performance or dance, writing, solving an equation, drawing or painting, storytelling, drama, or repairing a car. This stage requires a demonstration of text in a way that can be validated by others through the re-creation of meaning. She succinctly states this through her observation that *"literacy is a process of merging who we believe we are with what we show we can do."* This definition is very much in keeping with a holistic view of Vygotskyian development as becoming the text, not merely reading it. This notion of authoring parallels Moran and John-Steiner's description of Vygotsky's dialectic of internalization and externalization, which is the goal of learning in the ZPD. (Gallas, 2003, p. 100)

Internalization is not just copying but rather a transformation or reorganization of incoming information and mental structures based on the individual's characteristics and existing knowledge; internalization reflects not "content" poured into a person's psychological structure, it is how that structure is formed. Externalization is demonstrated when the individual explains the new skill or concept in his or her own words or way. (Moran & John Steiner, 2003, p. 63)

Mentoring in the ZPD

One of the most effective ways of mentoring in the Zone of Proximal Development can be described as helping students notice what they might not see on their own. This is partly accomplished through the expression of the mentor's enthusiasm and intellectual interest in the target area of study. This process has the potential to open students to Vygotsky's notion of "higher mental functions" and his work in the *Psychology of Art*. In the passage cited below, Vygotsky connects the social dimension of learning that is created in expressing art criticism in prose with all aspects of the human experience. (Vygotsky, 1997a)

The criticism which consciously and intentionally puts art into prose establishes its social root, and determines the social connection that exists between art and the general aspects of life. It gathers our conscious forces to counteract or, conversely, to cooperate with those impulses which have been generated by a work of art. This criticism leaves the domain of art and enters the sphere of social life, with the sole purpose of guiding the aesthetically aroused forces into socially useful channels. (Retrieved from: http://www.marxists.org/archive/vygotsky/works/1925/art11.htm)

Vygotsky goes on to discuss a situation that is strikingly similar to problems of education in our

day. The following citation describes learning *outside* the zone of proximal development.

> Until recently, the public approach to art prevailed in our schools as well as in our criticism. The students learned or memorized incorrect sociological formulas concerning many works of art. "At the present time," says Gershenzon, "pupils are beaten with sticks to learn Pushkin, as if they were cattle herded to the watering place, and given a chemical dissociation of H2o instead of drinking water." It would be unfair to conclude with Gershenzon that the system of teaching art in the schools is wrong from beginning to end. (ibid)

Vygotsky follows this by adding further points to his argument as to how art enjoyment and appreciation (or appreciation for anything) could be taught. What he describes here is the work of mentoring in the ZPD.

> The act of artistic creation cannot be taught. This does not mean, however, that the educator cannot cooperate in forming it or bringing it about. We penetrate the subconscious through the conscious. We can organize the conscious processes in such a way that they generate subconscious processes, and everyone knows that an act of art includes, as a necessary condition, all preceding acts of rational cognizance, understanding, recognition, association, and so forth. It is wrong to assume that the later subconscious processes do not depend on the direction imparted by us to the conscious processes.... The tremendous strength that arouses emotions, inspires the will, fortifies energy, and pushes us to action lies in the concreteness of the artistic image which is in turn based upon the originality of the psychological path leading to it. (ibid.)

This "psychological path" is socially constructed and although as many have stated "it cannot be taught," as many others put it, "it can be

caught." To better understand the process mentioned above by Vygotsky, we turn to Eliot Eisner's concepts of "teacher as a midwife to perception" and the significance of educational connoisseurship. (Eisner, 1998, p. 6)

In the midwife metaphor, the teacher helps to give birth to internalized meaning and externalized expression and, at the same time, challenges the learner to greater quality through appropriate criticism. Eisner points out that "effective criticism functions as the midwife to perception. It helps it come into being, then later refines it and helps it to become more acute." In keeping with the midwife metaphor, individual care and concern and an awareness of the process of organic time in the learner is of primary concern. By this, we are not referring to the discipline of lifespan developmental psychology as taught by Piaget and others. The zone of proximal development is a relationship between the teacher and the learner wherein both teacher and learner exercise reflective, critical and generative thinking and practice to discover, express and evaluate desired learning. (Eisner, 1998, p. 6)

The convergence of both the creative and critical aspects of learning brings us to another metaphor of the teacher that should be included. This is the notion of the teacher as a connoisseur. This role is important "in any realm in which the character, import, or value of objects, situations, and performances is distributed and variable, including educational practice." (p. 63) The critic is the public side of the same role. "Connoisseurs simply need to appreciate what they encounter. Critics, however, must render these qualities vivid, by the artful use of critical disclosure." By presenting connoisseurship and criticism as two aspects of the same concept, Eisner supports a creative-critical aspect of the zone of proximal development that helps to recognize and distinguish finely nuanced aspects of learning in every domain of inquiry. The critical aspect is the public expression of connoisseurship that involves the communication of de-

tailed distinctions in such a way that they are recognized and understood by others. (Eisner, 1998, p. 63; Eisner, 1985, pp. 92–93)

For an example of this process at work, we present the narrative of member of a rock band as he describes being awakened to the genius of one of the greatest yet relatively unknown bass guitar players of all time. His example provides us with a salient use of educational connoisseurship, because the bass line of a song is, for the most part, difficult to perceive to the untrained ear.

> "Listen man, that's James Jamerson!" one of the band members said. Sure enough, instead of the usual "boom boomp" of the standard bass line, what was being played was a distinct counter melody itself. Forty years later, I am still fascinated by Jamerson's genius on the instrument. After being taught to notice what I might not have been aware of otherwise, I am always eager to share what I have learned. Now, I tell my children to listen for nuances in the bass line all the time.

This same notion of connoisseurship and criticism could be used to cause others to notice anything, from the practical uses of the Pythagorean theory, to the power of propaganda, or the perspective of sunlight in fine art, to the subtle differences in the taste of butter from different geographical regions. The connoisseur-critic is certainly an essential feature of a mentor in the zone of proximal development.

Assessment in the Zone of Proximal Development

The way that assessment is performed in the ZPD provides another clear example of the contrast with being in or out of the zone. In traditional classroom assessment, the goal is the attainment of a singular measurable product such as a test score or a "benchmark" that is the result of the use of a standardized test. Instead, teachers should be open to many dif-

ferent kinds of assessment to insure that the student has truly internalized and externalized the content through means of the ZPD. Dot Robbins writes about assessment that brings into view the whole personality of the child within the ZPD.

> *Dynamic Assessment* is a new form of interweaving teaching-with-testing with learning. There is often a pre-test, then an "intervention" (which can be called "mediation"), and a post-test. Within Vygotskian non-classical psychology, the pupil/student is viewed as a *whole personality*, with the teacher helping motivate each person related to the test that is given. Then, there are sessions to help correct the problem areas, and the student is then retested. (2011, p. 20)

These assessments can range from encouraging a preschool child "to show what she knows to having a committee meeting for a doctoral candidate that combines oral and written assessment in a setting that most certainly should be a ZPD. If not, then the candidate needs to search for new committee personnel." (Bodrova & Leong, 1996, p. 40)

Another promising method of teaching and assessment in the ZPD comes from the Met Center in Providence, Rhode Island, USA. In this high school, students seek out community mentors in real work communities. There are cooperating mentors from a vast range of specialized employment areas in everything from fashion design to film editing, auto mechanics, teaching, health professions, music and dance performance, veterinarian assistants, floral arrangements and building trades. Students spend two days a week out of the classroom, shadowing their mentors and actually helping on the job. Their assessment experience is described on their website.

> The MET regards assessment as a learning tool that is woven throughout the teaching and learning process. The main goals of assessment are to help the student reflect on his or her work, create strate-

gies to improve, and develop his or her own internal standards. Evaluation processes should be learning experiences within themselves, strengthening the quality of students' work and their understanding of themselves as learners. The use of multiple assessment tools is vital to determine a student's progress and finding creative solutions to help students build on strengths and address gaps. The whole student must be addressed, looking at each project and activity in light of the student's personal learning plan. MET students learn to reflect on their work with the question, "Is it good enough?" the work is measured against standards of the real world held by the mentor and internship worksite as well as the exhibition panel. Everyone involved in the student's life and learning—including their family, peers and mentors—is asked to participate in the evaluation process. The MET's key elements for student assessments include: exhibitions; digital portfolios; narratives; and, transcripts. (Retrieved from: http://metcenter.org/the-education/evaluation/)

Undoubtedly this kind of schooling is more of what Vygotsky envisioned as the dialectical process of teaching and learning. For him, learning should never be reduced to a completed product, but it must always focus on the process of *becoming* what one desires to learn instead of learning in decontextualized isolation.

Glossary

Activity theory—In Vygotsky's work, this refers to deliberate and purposeful actions that are performed with the goals of bringing the actor(s) from mere biologically adaptive functioning to higher levels of consciousness, thinking and being. In the student driver example, some of the activities include pretend driving, playing driver video games and driving the dual-controlled driver's training car.

Behaviorism—is a school of psychology that is focused on measurable and observable behaviors in subjects that are

motivated by external stimuli and operant conditioning. In educational contexts, behaviorism views learning as a set of habits acquired in individualized and measured with standardized methods of testing.

Deficit model of schooling—A view of education that is focused on negative expectations of students derived from stereotypes of ethnicity and socio-economic status or disabilities. The curriculum is often focused on "remediation."

Eugenics—is a word that was created by Francis Galton to refer to the science of human reproduction that has as its goal the "improvement" of the human species through selective breeding and population control. The work of the American eugenics movement was praised and adopted by Adolf Hitler in his quest to create a "master race." Vygotsky's view of development presents a vital counterpoint to this theory.

Obuchenie—The Russian word for education that unlike the English word, which separates the function of teaching and learning, instead means that there is a mutual dependence and intertwining of teacher and learner in one holistic process.

Prolepsis—The perception of an anticipated or future condition of development before it actually exists as an internalized state of being.

Scaffolding—refers to the temporary use of instructional support that provides the learner ease of access to the targeted zones of the subject matter until it becomes internalized.

Zone of Proximal Development—The developmental space between a learner's actual and potential levels of thinking, problem solving, acting and being.

Vygotsky's View of the Dialectical Relationship between Thinking and Speech

Word meaning is a phenomenon of thought only insofar as thought is embodied in speech, and of speech only insofar as speech is connected with thought and illuminated by it. It is a phenomenon of verbal thought, of meaningful speech—a union of word and thought. (Vygotsky, 1986, p. 212)

When you are thinking about something do you ever find yourself pondering visually without accompanying words? Or do you sometimes find that you have to "translate" words or phrases into mental images before you can understand them? This is certainly the case for a leading advocate in autism research, Temple Grandin. In fact she says that "words are like a second language to me." As she reflects on her life as an autistic person she writes of an amazing self-discovery. (2006, p. 3)

One of the most profound mysteries of autism has been the remarkable ability of most autistic people to excel at visual spatial skills while performing so poorly at verbal skills. When I was a child and a teenager, I thought everybody thought in pictures. I had no idea that my thought processes were different. In fact, I did not realize the full extent of the differences until very recently. At meetings and at work I started asking other people detailed questions about how they accessed information from their memories. From their answers I learned that my visualization skills far exceeded those of most other people. (ibid)

As we consider Grandin's personal discovery, the possibilities for education are rich in both directions of internalization and externalization of language and thought. As we saw in one of the examples in the last chapter, Tonya Perry's students could parrot the vocabulary from *The Diary of Anne Frank*, but until the exploratory drama session took place empathetic connections to the story were almost non-existent.

These examples will hopefully enable us to understand Vygotsky's holistic view of the dialectical relationship between thinking and speaking. At this point we need to remember that Vygotsky did not view dialectical relationships as a cut and dried "thesis, antithesis, synthesis" swing of a pendulum. Instead he was able to hold opposing ideas together in paradox and always as a non-static process. This is illustrated through the revision of his most popular book *Thought and Language*. This was the title given to the first English translation of his work in 1962. But by 1987 the complete version was retitled as *Thinking and Speech* in order to express Vygotsky's view that thinking and speaking are active processes not dead nouns. This is confirmed in one of those richly expressive passages in Vygotsky's work that it will take the rest of this chapter to explain. (Newman & Holzman, 1993, p. 111)

The relationship of thought to word is not a thing but a process, a movement from thought to word and from word to thought . . . Thought is not expressed but completed in the word. We can, therefore, speak of the establishment (i.e., the unity of being and nonbeing) of thought in the word. . . . The structure of speech is not simply the mirror image of the structure of thought. It cannot, therefore, be placed on thought like clothes off a rack. Speech does not merely serve as the expression of developed thought. Thought is restructured as it is transformed into speech. It is not expressed but completed in the word. (Vygotsky, 1987e, pp. 250–251)

In order to illustrate the monistic unity of thought and word and the interplay that exists in the absence of a the mirror image and clothes rack metaphor that Vygotsky used in the above passage, we will consider the role of private, inner and outer speech, the use of speech genres and discourse, linguistic relativity, writing as an extension of reading and thinking, and metaphor use in concept formation. These terms are all examples of Vygotsky's use of language as the premier form of cultural tools for the development of higher levels of consciousness. Vygotsky and his colleagues all agree that for the most part "language separates humans from animal, making humans much more efficient as problem solvers." (Bodrova & Leong, 1996, p. 95)

At this point there are some terms (good example of language as tools) used in Vygotskian studies that we need to know if we are to grasp the vital role that Vygotsky placed on language in development. The terms listed below should not be viewed as separate but all interdependent and holistic processes of development.

All of three of these terms are integral parts of what is called Vygotsky's **genetic** method of which the processes involved in thinking and speaking are all central in the development of higher mental

Ontogenesis

From the Greek words "onto," which means being, and "genesis," meaning origin. This is a term used by Vygotsky to describe the unfolding of individual human development as a process of both biological and social forces (see end of the chapter for more).

Phylogenesis

From the Greek word "phylo" meaning tribe. A term used by Vygotsky that refers to the evolution of the human family. Of course he saw this not only as a biological process, but as the product of social formation mediated through the use of language, which distinguishes humans from apes whom he viewed as "slaves of the situation." (cited in Wertsch, 1991, p. 20)

functioning. Each of the topics discussed below express distinct yet united language processes.

Vygotsky revised Piaget's notion of egocentric speech or self-talk to a more focused concept that "is particularly powerful when children confront challenging tasks. When a child relies on audible speech while struggling with hard problems, the child develops a form of language that is somewhat different from speech addressed communicatively to others." This is called **private speech**. Vygotsky believed that it plays a vital role in more difficult problem solving tasks in children. "The more complex the action, demanded by the situation and the less direct its solution, the greater the importance played by speech as a whole." It is clear to all of you reading, however, that private speech is not limited to children. Adults use it in problem solving all the time. For example this works well when you retrace your steps while talking to yourself as you look for a lost item. (John-Steiner, 2007, p. 138; Vygotsky & Luria, cited in John-Steiner, 2007, p. 139)

In the case of children, Laura Berk concluded from her study of children in grades 1–3 that private speech is used in the classroom continuously. In fact she stated that "every child we observed talked to himself or herself, on average, 60% of the time." One of the not so surprising conclusions of Berk's research was that "first graders who made many self guiding comments out loud or quietly did better at second grade math. (ibid.) In math computation this goes right along with counting on your fingers or dots, so it makes sense that it happens frequently. (1994, p. 81)

In more recent studies, Berk (2004) shared other astute examples of private or self-talk as a continuation of Vygotsky's view that thinking and speaking are interconnected. These examples support Vygotsky's view of private speech as a "means of internal activity aimed at mastering oneself."(Vygotsky, 1978, p. 55)

- Two-year-old Peter experiments with language sounds, structures, and meanings as he

---

Private speech

is self-directed for the purpose of self-regulation and problem solving. Private speech functions in the threshold between outward communication and inner speech and is distinct from inner speech in many ways, yet all of these aspects of language overlap.

sings to himself, "Put the mushroom on your head. Put the mushroom in your pocket. Put the mushroom on your nose." Then, as he eyes his cat Tony, he exclaims, "Put the mushroom on the Tony," and laughs.

- While counting raisins at snack time, 5-year-old Carla says out loud rapidly, "One-two-three-four-five!" Then she continues more slowly, "Six, seven, eight, nine. Nine raisins!" she emphasizes, with satisfaction.

- Standing in front of an easel, 4-year-old Omar picks up a brush, then stops and surveys other nearby easels. "Where's the green? I need some green," he remarks, apparently referring to the missing green paint, which had been at the easels the day before.

- In his second-grade class, Tommy reads the text before him aloud, sounding out a hard-to-decipher name. "Sher-lock Holmlock, Sherlock Holme," he says, leaving off the final "s" in his second, more successful attempt.

- Three-year-old Rachel leans against the wall, looks down, and mumbles to herself, "Mommy's sick, Mommy's sick," in an apparent effort to come to terms with this stressful event. (Berk, 2004, p. 94)

Microgenesis
This term is used in Vygotskian studies to refer to "the unfolding of a single psychological act (for instance the act of perception, often over the course of milliseconds" (ibid., p. 23). This involves targeting specific areas of development such as learning language tasks or solving a specific problem.

All of these examples express the value of private speech in **microgenetic** applications to specific areas of learning, including emotional self-regulation in the last example. There is immense educational value in private speech that should not be overlooked in today's climate of standardized schooling and even standardized childhood.

For example, Berk presents other stories of English language learners actually practicing sophisticated changes in sentence structures during what has been deemed and greatly misunderstood as the "silent period" in second language acquisition. They often practice their responses in private speech, as in the case of a 5½-year-old Japanese stu-

dent who practiced the following in private speech before taking the risks to speak aloud in class.

"I finished, I have finished, I am finished, I'm finished ... I want, I paper. Paper. Paper. I want paper." Through private speech this boy was able to engage in transformative self-regulation of English grammar. Berk goes on to say that the "silent period" was "not silent at all." (Berk, 2004, p. 95; Krashen, 1990, p. 72.)

Yet many students have been misdiagnosed during this silent phase, resulting in many being misplaced in special education where they often experience what we referred to in the last chapter as deficit schooling that produces deficit expectations, which becomes a manifestation of a zone of arrested development instead of a ZPD. In her stunning book *The Inner World of the Immigrant Child,* Cristina Igoa (1995) shares out of her rich experience that the silent phase should be viewed in a much more positive light than some critics believe who consider it to be a waste of time and instead emphasize the "sink or swim" approach. In contrast to this Igoa sees the need for an incubation period. This concept is very much in keeping with Vygotsky's view of thought and language merging through a process rather than a product.

> While some are trapped in helpless silence by their inability to communicate in the dominant language, they become insightful observers of their own human condition and of life around them. In that silence, they develop strong listening skills; they come to value keenly language as a mode of self-expression; they do not take language for granted because of the time in their lives when they were silent. Then they experience the sheer joy of breaking that silence. (p. 38)

Berk shares another powerful example of private speech at work (or should I say at play) which can be seen in the form of children creating imaginary

playmates. Berk sees this as much more than self-entertainment for bored children. "Dialogues with make-believe partners may serve a special coping function, offering a safe context in which to practice social skills with nonthreatening 'playmates' before transferring them to the real world of peer play." Some parents and teachers have bought into the idea that such activities should be restricted or stopped altogether. (Berk, 2004, p. 96)

One story comes from two sisters who shared an imaginary playmate named Speedy Harbor. These two girls were often cared for by their aunt since the parent's work involved quite a bit of travel. The aunt decided that the girls were spending too much time with the imaginary playmate so one day she told the girls that Speedy Harbor had died. Needless to say they were really upset by this news so they decided to have a funeral for Speedy Harbor by placing him in a shoebox and burying him. Years later one of the sisters told this story to her classmates in an undergraduate psychology class and of course the professor was horrified.

According to Berk, "25–45 percent of 3–7 year olds have at least one imaginary friend, and many more than one." Other estimates are higher. For example Taylor, Carlson, Maring, Gerow, and Charley reported that "overall, 65% of children up to the age of 7 had imaginary companions at some point during their lives." Further research is needed in this area but as of this moment in 2011, it is clear that imaginary friends for the most part play a positive role in social processes of development and language internalization. The next area we shall consider is **inner speech**. This serves as a distinct function to private speech but represents another facet of Vygotsky's view of thinking and speaking as separate yet complementary functions. "Inner speech is not the interior aspect of external speech-it is a function in itself." (Berk, 2004, p. 97; Taylor, Carlson, Maring, Gerow, & Charley, p. 1, abstract; Vygotsky, 1986, p. 249)

Inner Speech
refers to a unique form of inner dialogue with oneself comprised of both speech and "a distinct plane of verbal thought (which is) comprised of pure meaning." (Vygotsky, 1986, pp. 248–249) (See end of chapter for more.)

The Formation of Inner Speech

The process of inner speech formation brings us once again to this quote from Vygotsky (1978).

> Every function in the child's cultural development appears twice: first, on the social level, and later, on the individual level; first, between people (interpsychological) and then inside the child (intrapsychological). This applies equally to voluntary attention, to logical memory, and to the formation of concepts. All the higher functions originate as actual relationships between individuals. (p. 57)

This richly loaded thought is accompanied in the text with an illustration of a child learning the true meaning of the pointing gesture. Meaningful communication occurs "only after it objectively manifests all the functions of pointing for others and is understood by others as such a gesture." However in keeping with the central theme of process in all of Vygotsky's work, it is important to acknowledge each step of internalization. For example, an eighteen-month-old child may wave at everything they like and as a form of communication with others. In the context of inner speech formation, first the child sees others pointing, then imitates. This is followed by internalization and ultimately by external communication when the practical needs are present, like "I want *that* juice." (ibid, p. 56)

Inner speech follows the same route of socialization, imitation and internalization and "has both social and cultural roots," meaning that it is shaped by a particular culture, place and time with the social setting. We will look into this further in a discussion of the cultural relativity of language. Individual factors also play a role as in the case of Temple Grandin and autism. The unique properties of each person's inner landscape create endless variety in the forms of inner speech and processes of thought. Inner speech is the sum and substance of personal identity and therefore with agency.

(Vocate, 1994, p. 16) Oliver Sacks (1989) astutely observes:

> Our real identity lies in inner speech, in that ceaseless stream and generation of meaning that constitutes the individual mind. It is through inner speech that the child develops his own identity; it is through inner speech, finally that he constructs his own world. (p. 73)

Now we come to the heart of Vygotsky's emphasis on personal agency through inner speech leading to internalized connections that finds articulation through multiple discourses and genres, including numeracy, drama, music, dance, graphic and fine art, literature, craftsmanship, invention, agriculture, technology, athletics, and all forms of outward communication. Again the process is summarized by social communication leading inner speech and concept formation, followed by external expression in shared meanings. What then are some of the ways that individualized inner speech occurs? In specific terms, what are some examples from biographical history that might help us to understand ways to help recognize ways that personal agency and voice is created? Vera John-Steiner is a prominent voice in the field of Vygotskian scholarship who has devoted many years of research on these questions. One salient aspect to her inquiry is that it may be hard "to specify the nature of a person's inner language. Its description and identification may be indirectly determined by how one gathers and remembers experience." Indeed people internalize experience through a myriad of both formal and informal activities within and without school settings including play, work, and every form of social activity. Some individuals experience the world primarily through visual means. Others possess the ability to recall verbal conversations or specific dates. Others remember saliently through sounds or smells or muscle memory. These do not function in isolation from each other, nor is it wise to label them as specific "intelli-

gences" in a way that might limit rather than expand one's self-awareness. We just are who we are with diverse ways of experiencing and being in the world. There is not adequate space in this book or in many volumes to cover all these diverse ways of experiencing the world, especially when you consider the immense variety of forms of communication. Take sign language for example. Oliver Sacks writes that communication in Sign (capitalized because this it is now an official language in many countries) has the power to change the structure of the brain "as it develops a wholly new capacity to 'linguisticize' space (or to spatialize language)." Now, twenty years after Sacks wrote this, this statement has been confirmed by PET scan imaging through research conducted by Emmorey and McCullough (2009). Work of this sort provides us with another example of how Vygotsky's writing is still full of possibilities for present and future research in the social development, internalization and externalization of language and thought. (John-Steiner, 1985, p. 213; Sacks, 1989, pp. 114, 115)

Visual Inner Speech

Visual thinking is one of the foremost sources of creativity and yet it is also one of the most neglected in schools today. One reason may be because mental images and other forms of inner speech are much harder to quantify and generalize to an entire group of students. Yet it is clear visual inner speech has the potential to play a role in the discovery process of every content area. One of the classic examples of this is from the mathematical-scientific domain in the life of Albert Einstein. It is important to remember that he sensed that much was missing in some of the prevailing theories of physics that were espoused by Sir Isaac Newton. His questions led him to episodes of deeply imagining against the grain of these popular views for more than ten years. This ultimately led him to a breakthrough year of discovery

in 1905. His breakthrough, of course, was focused on his theory of relativity, which happened by picturing himself riding through space on a light wave while "looking" back at the wave next to him. I think we would be hard put to find someone else in history who could claim a similar experience with those images. Apparently, Einstein only saw the need to think in words in a secondary stage after working out his concepts in a way that he could reproduce them at any time. (Orman, 1995) Here is what he wrote about this notion in a letter to the mathematician Hadamard (1945):

> The words or the language, as they are written or spoken, do not seem to play any role in my mechanism of thought. The psychical entities which seem to serve as elements in thought are certain signs and more or less clear images which can be "voluntarily" reproduced and combined. There is, of course, a certain connection between those elements and relevant logical concepts. It is also clear that the desire to arrive finally at logically connected concepts is the emotional basis of this rather vague play with the above-mentioned elements. But taken from a psychological viewpoint, this combinatory play seems to be the essential feature in productive thought—before there is any connection with logical construction and words or other kinds of signs which can be communicated to others. The above-mentioned elements are, in any case, some of visual and some of muscular types. Conventional words or other signs have to be sought laboriously only in a secondary stage, when the mentioned associative play is sufficiently established and can be reproduced at will. (pp. 142–143)

One reason that visual thinking has not been the focus of school curriculum is because in cultures that equate school success primarily with standardized test scores that are driven by behaviorism, there is very little comparative space and time given for

the cultivation of interior phenomena. In contrast to this, scholars of the Gestalt psychology philosophy have led the way in giving credibility to imagistic thought. In Gestaltist writings, "thought and sight are dynamically interconnected." John-Steiner goes on to say that visual thinking has advantages over some aspects of verbal thinking because the former has more fluidity and therefore it yields a "great diversity of graphic and plastic means used by creative individuals in shaping and communicating their inner visual notions." As a whole, we are not harnessing these advantages in schools because expression of this variety is harder to control and assess. Breakthroughs of comprehension and discovery across every content area might very well be waiting in the cultivation of imagistic thinking provided by the domain of the arts and more hands-on approaches to learning that are rich with visual content and experience. (John-Steiner, 1985, pp. 85–86)

Inner speech in motion

In the above citation, Einstein refers not only to visual thought but also to "muscular types" of thought or what might be called thought in motion. In the example from Einstein's breakthrough discovery, visual imagery is conjoined with kinesthetic imagery as he rides a beam of light backward while looking over at another moving beam. The movement in this expression of inner speech provides a means to capture the essence of relativity that words and even visual thought alone could not provide. Consider again the example of sign language. It is not just visual but also involves movement or body thinking as it shapes the moving thinkers brain through body-mind connections.

The implications for education are very clear. Students learn much less when they are inert and focused only on a narrow range of cognition. Instead of cultivating higher forms of consciousness as

Vygotsky envisioned through the signs and tools of language, this disembodied methodology is responsible for creating quite the opposite. In this present situation, if children are not able to sit still for 6 to 7 hours a day to take in more language, we drug them with Ritalin. We need a revolution of movement in schools from kindergarten all the way up through graduate schools of education. We talk about the need for creative and critical thinking, but we starve our children of the environments needed to inspire and cultivate the kind of visual and kinesthetic inner speech mentioned here.

Richard Louv is one of the primary voices for a growing movement called *No Child Left Inside.* I am sure that if Vygotsky were alive today it would be hard to for him to grasp the fact that so many of the children in the world are sent outside and taken away from computers, games and TV as a form of corrective discipline. Even forty years ago, the opposite was true! In his wonderful book, *Last Child in the Woods,* Louv (2008) masterly describes a condition he calls "nature deficit disorder" (p. 10) as the real and viable antidote to ADHD. Later in the book he cites a story from *San Francisco* magazine which serves as a powerful case study to the process of internalization and transformation through visual-kinesthetic inner speech and external expression of the highest order.

> The back page of an October issue of *San Francisco* magazine displays a vivid photograph of a small boy, eyes wide with excitement and joy, leaping and running on a great expanse of California beach, storm clouds and towering waves behind him. A short article explains that the boy was hyperactive, he had been kicked out of his school, and his parents had not known what to do with him—but they had observed how nature engaged and soothed him. So for years they took their son to beaches, forests, dunes, and rivers to let nature do its work. The photograph was taken in 1907. The boy was Ansel Adams. (pp. 102–103)

This story also provides us with a glimpse of the inherent potential within a customized zone of proximal development created by Adams' parents as they exposed him to a rich variety of natural settings that developed his inner sense of beauty and form that is present in the rhythm and movement of the natural world. It was indeed the inner eye without the help of the kind of advanced technology we have today that enabled Adams to create his stunning work. In an interview by John Husker for the 1989 film *Ansel Adams: Photographer*, Adams recalled:

> Well, people have asked me what kind of cameras I used. It's hard to remember all of them. Oh, I had a box Brownie #1 in 1915, 16. I had the Pocket Kodak, and a 4 x 5 view, all batted down. I had a Zeiss Milliflex. A great number of different cameras. I want to try to get back to 35 millimeter, which I did a lot of in the 1930s, using one of the Zeiss compacts. In the 20s and into the 30s, I would carry a 6-1/2 x 8-1/2 glass plate camera—that was a little heavy. And I had a 4 x 5 camera, then of course we went to film, to film pack, things became a little simpler. (Gray & Huszar, 1989)

None of these kinds of thinking exists in isolation. Ideally, they can all work together as they shape and are shaped by one another. Multiple modes of inner speech can lead to the discovery of personal identity through the connections it creates when it is joined with outer communication through the **mediation** of language and shared meaning.

> Language is a bridge between individuals who wish to overcome divisions born of the diversity of human experience. It is also a bridge between inner thought and shared understanding: the past and the present, the world of the senses and the realm of thought. (John-Steiner, 1985, p. 111)

Before we move into more detail about how the connections between outer and inner language are

---

Mediation

using a sign, symbol, or gesture that generates higher mental processes. For Vygotsky these almost always involved the use of language. A simple example can be found in the word "hot," which means "do not touch or you will experience pain." A more developed mediatory sign could be a parent offering their son or daughter the keys to the family car, which mediates trust and responsibility.

created through concept formation, we need to elaborate further on the features of inner speech. This will be accomplished by summarizing Johnson's elaboration on inner speech. (1994, pp. 176–179)

- Inner speech is subvocal and generative. It is silent because it is internal but it is much than more private thinking because it is strongly abbreviated and generative since it contains thoughts in seed form. "A thought may be compared to a cloud shedding a shower of words." (Vygotsky, 1986, p. 251)
- Inner speech is arranged in "syntactical ellipsis" (p. 177), meaning that it is incomplete or abbreviated. Vygotsky says that in inner speech "a single word is so saturated with sense that many words would be required to explain it in external speech." (p. 148) For example someone might use a metaphor like "bike wheel" in inner speech to describe something with many spokes stemming out from a hub.
- Inner speech has semantic embeddedness (p. 178). This refers again to the "extreme elliptical economy of inner speech which is known only to the inner speech thinker." An example might be thinking one word such as "yes!" which might take thousands of words in outward speech to describe what the thinker is feeling so positive about. (Vygotsky, 1962, p. 45)
- Inner speech is egocentric (p. 179). This does not necessarily mean greedy or egotistical. This refers to the fact that the inner speaker does not have to address their thoughts for an audience or assume the viewpoint of another person.

All of these characteristics of inner speech together become meaningful communication when they are joined to language or speech. The union of thought and word in Vygotsky's view involves the

process of concept formation. Next we will provide an overview of his theory of how this occurs.

Concept Formation

As we ponder the way the Vygotsky viewed concept formation it is important to remember that he viewed the origin of the entire process as one that is socially constructed, that is, from the outside in, rather than from the inside out. The distinction is important from the standpoint of whether one believes, as Noam Chomsky and the mentalist school of psychology teaches, that humans possess hardwiring for language acquisition that unfolds in a series of individualized stages of Piagetian development. Vygotsky saw concept development in stages as well, but the emphasis in his view was not as biologically based as Piaget and, much later, Chomsky. In Vygotsky's view of concept formation, he lists these processes as "syncretic heaps" followed by thinking in "complexes," which he divides in the following types: "associative, collective, chain, diffuse and pseudo concepts." These two phases lead to the third phase—concept formation. We will briefly touch on each of these aspects while giving more attention to concept formation since for pedagogical purposes, it requires the most attention. (Vygotsky, 1986, pp. 110–111; Vygotsky, 1986, pp. 111–124).

Syncretic Heaps

At around 2–3 years old, children discover connections between objects by trial and error. When a child discovers that two things do not belong together, another object is brought in to replace one of them. This stage is highly subjective and driven by what the child might feel belongs together, rather than what the actual name of the object might be. This is refined somewhat as the child

learns to distinguish themselves from the world around them through the organization of their field of vision as well as space and time perception. As with everything in Vygotsky's development theories, this is an overlapping process with no cut-and-dried separation at this point between the child's egocentric perception and reality.

Thinking in Complexes

Vygotsky defines thinking in complexes as a means "to establish bonds and relations. This begins with the unification of scattered impressions; by organizing discrete elements of experience into groups. This creates the basis for later generalizations." Complexes are distinct from syncretic heaps because they are less abstract and concrete because "they reflect certain features actually shared" between objects. (In the experiments conducted by Vygotsky, these objects were toy blocks.) (1986, p. 135; Kozulin, 1990, p. 160)

As we mentioned above, within the category of complexes, Vygotsky further recognizes five types: associative, collective, chain, diffuse and pseudo-concepts. An associative complex shares distinctive features in some way but may still be separate from other categories. For example the child may link pictures of a black cat and a black shoe together. Collective complexes are based on observations of "objects together in their concrete functional context." An example of this is when a child recognizes that hand tools go together in a tool box. (van der Veer & Valsiner, 1991, p. 264).

The next complex that Vygotsky mentions is a chain, which he says "is the purest form of thinking in complexes" *because* "the end of the chain may have nothing in common with the beginning." For example a child can start out by connecting cherries and raisins together because they are both sweet fruit but then switch the connection based on another link which seems to miss a few steps, when

the cherries become the eyes and the raisins form the mouth of a snowman. The diffuse complex occurs when children generalize about associations of objects or images "because of a dim impression that they have something in common" (ibid). The example that Vygotsky uses for this type of complex is a connection between triangles and trapezoids "because they made him thinks of triangles with their tops cut off." (Vygotsky, 1986, pp. 117, 118)

Vygotsky goes on to to say that complexes of this sort are limitless and expansive as in the case of shapes when the next connections "lead to squares then hexagons" and then "different colored ones." This endless variation is the result of "surprising transitions, of startling associations and generalizations." This is different from a logical chain and actually shows more fluidity of thought. (Vygotsky, 1986, p. 118)

The last type of complex that Vygotsky mentions is called a pseudoconcept. This serves as a bridge between complexes and developed conceptual thinking. These two are very similar in some ways, but the main distinction is that a pseudoconcept is formed out of predetermined words learned "by the meaning a given word already has in the language of adults." In most cases the child learns many, many words from caregivers and yet this only opens the door to concept formation through the process of development. *In contrast, a concept is self-generated when the child is able to use words as tools of meaning making on their own and create rather that just acquire meaning from others.* (Vygotsky, 1986, p. 12)

When we consider Vygotsky's theory of concept formation in light of Freire's notion of critical pedagogy, there are many strong areas of convergence. We will discuss these in greater detail in the next chapter, but at this point it is interesting to note that Vygotsky's notion of "direct teaching" and Freire's metaphor of the "banking model of education" are similar constructs. Here Vygotsky shares that mere repetition of facts only touches the surface of learning.

Practical experience also shows that direct teaching of concepts is impossible and fruitless. A teacher who tries to do this usually accomplishes nothing but empty verbalism, a parrotlike repetition of words by the child, simulation knowledge of the corresponding concepts but actually covering up a vacuum. (Vygotsky, 1986, p. 150)

In language that is quite similar, Freire describes static "learning" as recording information, memorizing and repeating it, by using the metaphor of a student as an empty passive receptacle.

The teacher talks about reality as if it were motionless, static, compartmentalized, and predictable. Or else he expounds on a topic completely alien to the existential experience of the students. His task is to "fill" the students with the contents of his narration—contents which are detached from reality, disconnected from the totality that engendered them and could give them significance. Words are emptied of their concreteness and become a hollow, alienated, and alienating verbosity. The outstanding characteristic of this narrative education, then, is the sonority of words, not their transforming power. "Four times four is sixteen; the capital of Para is Belem." The student records, memorizes, and repeats these phrases without perceiving what four times four really means, or realizing the true significance of "capital" in the affirmation "the capital of Para is Belem," that is, what Belem means for Para and what Para means for Brazil. Narration (with the teacher as narrator) leads the students to memorize mechanically the narrated account. Worse yet, it turns them into "containers," into "receptacles" to be "filled" by the teachers. The more completely she fills the receptacles, the better a teacher she is. The more meekly the receptacles permit themselves to be filled, the better students they are. Education thus becomes an act of depositing, in which the students are the depositories and the teacher is the depositor. Instead of communicating,

the teacher issues communiques and makes deposits which the students patiently receive, memorize, and repeat. (Freire, 1970/2003, pp. 71–72)

Both Vygotsky and Freire view knowledge as constructed and dynamic rather than assimilated and static factual information that has not been self-generated through concept formation. They also both see the role of problem solving (Freire calls it problem posing) in this type of learning. Here Freire mentions a keyword in Vygotsky's theory of concept formation: intentionality. "Problem posing education, responding to the essence of consciousness—intentionality—rejects communiqués and embodies communication." External, isolated information, what Freire refers to here as "communiqués" are like being given a diagram for a dance step without actually and *intentionally* dancing with another person. We are reminded of the domain of the ZPD, which again is the "actual developmental level as determined by independent problem solving and the level of potential development as determined through problem solving under adult guidance or in collaboration with more capable peers." Whether the problem is learning to dance or learning to talk to a nurse in an emergency room in a second language, intentional and directed dialogue in shared meaning is required. So let's summarize before we look more closely at concept formation. (Freire, 1970/2003, p. 79; Vygotsky, 1986, p. 86)

A complex including a pseudoconcept is formed out of predetermined word meanings through social interaction. Concepts are formed through firsthand personal connections in creating meaning. The process of moving from heaps to concepts defines the space in the zone of proximal development. Yet this is not a pure linear trajectory, it is more like Bruner's notion of a spiral. He says that a "curriculum as it develops should revisit these basic ideas repeatedly, building upon them until the student has grasped the full formal apparatus that goes with them." Ideally this spiral metaphor will con-

tinue to move into higher levels of thought like a spiral staircase moving upward in the developmental process of consciousness. (Bruner, 1977, p. 13)

Scientific and Spontaneous Concepts

Vygotsky divided conceptual thinking into two types: scientific and spontaneous. These are separated for the purpose of definition, but in real life, they exist in a monistic process of experience and development. Spontaneous concepts are "are derived from people's direct experience with the world. The development of spontaneous concepts can be considered an inductive process." In educational terminology, we would could place spontaneous concepts in the domain of student's schema or background knowledge and "pattern recognition, comparisons made between multiple events, reflections on activities and the use of analogical reasoning." Spontaneous concepts move from the part to the whole through these kinds of connections. (Wellings, 2003, pp. 6–7) Vygotsky describes them as moving upward.

Scientific concepts on the other hand "can be considered a deductive process" that moves "downward" from the general to the specific through formal instruction to personal application. These two processes are inseparable in the ZPD in a spiraling movement toward internalization. A wise teacher will recognize and draw from both aspects. (Wellings, 2003, pp. 6–7)

Though scientific and spontaneous concepts develop in reverse directions, the two processes are closely connected. The development of a spontaneous concept must have reached a certain level for the child to be able to absorb a related scientific concept.... In working its slow way upward, an everyday concept clears a path for the scientific concept and its downward development. It creates a series of structures necessary for the evolution of

a concept's more primitive, elementary aspects, which give it body and vitality. Scientific concepts, in turn, supply structures for the upward development of the child's spontaneous concepts towards consciousness and deliberate use. Scientific concepts grow downward through spontaneous concepts; spontaneous concepts grow upward through scientific concepts. (Vygotsky, 1986, p. 194)

Vygotsky uses the example of teaching historical concepts (scientific) only when the child's (spontaneous) concept of the past is adequately formed. The process of development of higher consciousness is therefore a holistic blending of formal schooling and life experience. This sounds remarkably like another theorist who was influenced by Hegel, John Dewey, yet the two never read each other's work. It is worth reading this citation from Dewey here since it clearly describes the need for the integration of spontaneous and scientific concepts through a concerted emphasis on the equal value of educative experiences outside of the classroom as well as in it.

From the standpoint of the child, the great waste in the school comes from his inability to utilize the experiences he gets outside the school in any complete and free way within the school itself; while on the other hand, he is unable to apply in daily life what he is learning in school. That is the isolation of the school—its isolation from life. When the child gets into the schoolroom he has to put out of his mind a large part of the ideas, interests and activities that predominate in his home and neighborhood. So the school being unable to utilize this everyday experience sets painfully to work on another tack and by a variety of [artificial] means, to arouse in the child an interest in school studies. . . . . [Thus there remains a] gap existing between the everyday experiences of the child and the isolated material supplied in such large measure in the school. (1899/1956, pp. 75–76)

It is vitally important to look for ways to provide children with the kind of experiences that can release the entwining of spontaneous and scientific concepts. This is becoming more and more difficult in this era of standardized information that is to be "taught" according to Piagetian biological timetable of development. Steinberg astutely describes the problem with Piaget's generalizations of childhood to all children in every culture and period of history.

> Considering biological stages of child development fixed and unchangeable, teachers, psychologists, parents, welfare workers, and the community at large view children along a fictional taxonomy of development. Those children who don't "measure up" will be relegated to the land of low and self-fulfilling expectations." (2011, p. 3)

In the same context Steinberg mentions that before the Industrial Revolution, "children participated daily in the adult world, gaining knowledge of vocational and life skills as part of such engagement." The Age of Modernity brought in standardization and with it "the corporate construction of childhood."But one reason for the groundswell of interest in Vygotsky's work today is because he vehemently challenged these notions. (2011, pp. 2–3)

In his thickly described elaboration of how scientific concepts are developed, Vygotsky used the analogy of learning a foreign language. His main point is that both spontaneous and deliberate learning are inextricably united in the acquisition of a foreign language with "each system influencing the other and benefiting from the strong points of the other" in the formation of meaning. This example from a graduate student of Spanish as a foreign language, William Lake, may shed some light on the two aspects working together. (1986, p. 196)

He shared that when he thinks about how to express something in accurate meaning and structure and gender, he thinks back to where he first heard a phrase. Most of the time he remembers the very con-

versation and the setting in which he first heard the words or phrases used. By recalling the experience of spontaneous exposure, he was able to determine word gender and sentence level grammar in a way that draws on "scientific" conceptual learning. This experience supports Vygotsky's claim that "concepts do not lay in a child's mind like peas in a bag without any bonds between them. If that were the case no intellectual operation requiring coordination of thoughts would be possible." Thus Vygotsky's theory of education is based on conceptual blending of experience and directed learning through mediation. Before we go any further with examples of this, we need to discuss a few very important concepts in understanding Vygotsky's work. These terms will provide the basis for further discussion on thought and language. (Vygotsky, 1986, p. 197)

All of these terms operate within the dialectal processes of the internalization and external expression of thinking and speaking. In the example of Helen Keller, she could both accurately spell and "read" the spelling of her teacher through the mediation of signed spelling. In the **leading activity** involved in learning the scientific concept for water, the spontaneous experience of drinking water merged with it and finally the feeling of running water became an internalized **mediator** or mental tool that bridged thinking and speech for her. But the process did not stop there. She learned to read and became a prolific writer as well. This excerpt she wrote describes in rich detail her "school" experience. Children who can hear and see should have such sensually laden fabulous lessons from the real world every day of their lives.

> We read and studied out of doors, preferring the sunlit woods to the house. All my early lessons have in them the breath of the woods—the fine, resinous odour of pine needles, blended with the perfume of wild grapes. Seated in the gracious shade of a wild tulip tree, I learned to think that everything has a lesson and a suggestion. "The

Leading Activity
is a specifically guided activity that is created for the purpose of development. For example in the famous case involving Helen Keller, her teacher Anne Sullivan used sign language to spell w-a-t-e-r after placing Helen's hands under running water.

Mediator
Anything used in the process of mediation that, once internalized, becomes a mental tool. An example could be the alphabet song, which later helps in referencing alphabetical order.

loveliness of things taught me all their use." Indeed, everything that could hum, or buzz, or sing, or bloom had a part in my education—noisy-throated frogs, katydids and crickets held in my hand until forgetting their embarrassment, they trilled their reedy note, little downy chickens and wildflowers, the dogwood blossoms, meadow-violets and budding fruit trees. I felt the bursting cotton-bolls and fingered their soft fiber and fuzzy seeds; I felt the low soughing of the wind through the cornstalks, the silky rustling of the long leaves, and the indignant snort of my pony, as we caught him in the pasture and put the bit in his mouth—ah me! How well I remember the spicy, clovery smell of his breath. (1903, p. 23)

From Internalization to Communication

The above example is richly informative as an example of ways that internalized language becomes meaningful communication while making salient Vygotsky's ideas about the flexibility of thought and word. Through the mediation of vibration, fragrance, texture, temperature and shape, sound and scent became the words of inner speech. These thoughts merged with a desire to share her world with an audience. From this perspective of communicative intention, a poetic tone is released in sentences and paragraphs. In all Vygotsky has to say about language the ultimate goal is always making meaning for others in a community of thought. In this regard his ideas are similar to James Moffett's theories of discourse.

The fact that one writes by oneself does not at all diminish the need for response, since one writes for others. Even when one purports to be writing for oneself—for pure self-expression, if there is such a thing—one cannot escape the ultimately social implications inherent in any use of language. (1968, p. 191)

And so it is clear that language does not exist for private thoughts but for constructing and communicating meaning. Personal voice begins with internalized conceptual connections and finds articulation through "the universe of discourse" and John-Steiner's notion of "cognitive pluralism." Both of these concepts are parallel with Vygotsky's "examples of psychological and their complex systems; language; various systems for counting; mnemonic techniques; algebraic symbol systems; works of art; writing; schemes; diagrams; maps and mechanical drawings; all sorts of conventional signs; and so on." We should add drama, music, dance, literature, craftsmanship, invention, agriculture, technology, athletics, and all forms of communication. Students need to be encouraged to cultivate their own unique capacities in the same ways that the great creative minds used in these examples did. Some were visual thinkers; some thought best while moving; some of them needed to constantly touch the objects of inquiry. We have already mentioned the power of visual and kinesthetic thinking in the references to Einstein and Helen Keller. The following example of kinesthetic thinking and problem solving followed by a few lines of the verbal description of the process by the interviewee allows us to see how he "thinks" with his fingers. (Moffett, 1968; John-Steiner, 1995; Vygotsky, 1981, p. 137)

On a recent trip to North Carolina, I talked to a young man named Jason who dives in the muddy waters of the Dismal Swamp region, with hopes of finding Civil War artifacts. Of course there is zero visibility when one is completely submersed in mud. Jason has to rely completely on the sense of touch. As he finds submersed objects, he runs his fingers across the surfaces and his "fingers send a flash message to [his] brain." He can tell whether a bottle is antique or not by checking it for asymmetry, which would indicate that it was hand-blown glass. He reported with great enthusiasm how much fun it is to try and ascertain the identity of

unknown or unfamiliar objects through the sense of touch alone.

Jason's father created this zone of proximal development that served to co-construct this unusual capacity as they engaged in this activity together. There are millions of students in our schools today that are forced to sit for hours at a time and passively take in someone else's words. And for those who cannot sit still, we have lots of drugs, and if that does not work, we can put you in "alternative schools" or the "vocational track" often as a punitive measure for students with behavioral problems. In North America the fear of falling behind other countries academically and economically is often discussed at the same time as we continue to use a curriculum modeled after the kind that was used in tutoring 19th-century aristocratic males. Yet in many countries outside of North America, the lines between hands-on learning and academic subjects are very blurred or nonexistent and therefore there is much less stigma attached to vocational or technical training.

Auditory Thinking

There are many people who retain spoken language much better than written language. Their internalization process draws from the rhythm, inflection and emotional tone of spoken language. This notion led Coreil to question visually driven approaches to teaching English. Here is an account of a breakthrough that came out of his experiences of teaching English in Saudi Arabia.

"These guys cannot learn English," the Brit said. *"We have suggested dismissal, but the headmaster says no. Good luck and don't send any of them to my office, none, no matter what!"* So I went into the classroom, clicked my heels and said, "Hi! I'm Clyde." I drew not a smile. Forgetting what I had prepared, I proceeded to read them a simple story. They seemed to

quiet down. So I read it again and again each time, I asked simple questions about the story, and a couple of students blurted out very short and barely understandable but generally correct answers. Their **ears** had been working far better than their **tongues**. Anyway, later that afternoon, I recorded a couple of stories and copied the tapes one by one on my recorder. Then I wrote ten true false questions about the story. At the end of class next day, I handed out the tapes and exercises and gave them three days to finish. I did not include the printed version of the tape scripts.

After the three days, they had completed the assignment but were grumpy and implied that it was far too difficult... but asked where was the next one. They were even more upset when I said there was no next one, but that I would make another that afternoon and have it ready in a couple of days. If I hadn't, I fear that my motorcycle tires would have been sliced by a curved dagger. They weren't lazy. But many of them had grown up on the desert. They were fiercely independent and hated normal English class because it involved for them humiliation, embarrassment and frustration. On the other hand, the listening work was difficult, but they could do it. And they needed something they could be proud of. It was incredible to me how well they mimicked my tape-recorded voice: **"Oh, no," Ali said. "I can't go back there!"** I could hear traces of my Cajun accent in their voices. That class learned a lot of intonation, pronunciation and even grammar with me hardly ever mentioning it with my raspy voice. I am in no way a professional reader. I made up for this deficiency by hamming it up unashamedly and doing some slightly questionable things myself. For instance, I would pause occasionally and—breaking the narration—sternly say something like, "Abdul, wake up! This is not a tent!" Subsequently, in middle of class, one or another of them would repeat one of those admonitions in exactly the tone of voice I had used. So it wasn't only targeted speech production that they

learned, it was a number of aspects of speech patterns that I wasn't even aware that I had, much less had put on tape. I became more aware than ever of the great, extremely subtle interpretive powers of the human ear. If I had given them the printed tape script instead of the tapes, I don't think I would even remember the class now. Again, there's something very special about the human voice, the human ear, and the human imagination, and I am afraid that we are neglecting all three in many of our classrooms. (Coreil, 2007, pp. 160–161)

Numerical Thinking

In the movie *Rain Man* (1988) Dustin Hoffman gives a superb performance as an autistic savant that is based on the life of Kim Peek. Here is a little information about the life of the real Rain Man. Kim did not walk until age four. At that time he was also obsessed with numbers and arithmetic, reading telephone directories and adding columns of telephone numbers. He enjoyed totaling the numbers on automobile license plates as well. Since 1969 Kim has worked at a day workshop for adults with disabilities. Without the aid of calculators or adding machines, he has prepared information from work sheets for payroll checks. (Retrieved from: http://www.wisconsinmedicalsociety.org/savant/kimpeek)

The existence of people like Kim Peek suggests that there is a distinct inner language of numeracy. In fact, Einstein further stated in his letter to Hadamard that he expressed himself "in a different language, I think in mathematics." In my work as a literacy teacher, I have witnessed many students who did well in math computation, but not as well in reading comprehension. One reason for this is because many of the word problems are removed from the context of real life outside of schools. (Hadamard, 1945, p. 45)

Gutstein is working to remedy this situation by combining the language of math with issues of so-

cial justice. As a student of Michael Apple, Gutstein was strongly exposed to Freire's work and others in the pedagogy of critical consciousness. As a math teacher, he sought for ways to apply these concepts. He accomplishes this through problem-posing projects such as studying the mortgage loan rejection rate ratios by ethnicity in a number of U.S. cities. Another interesting project involves the cost of a B-2 bomber, "$44,754,000,000 for 21 planes," compared to the cost of college tuition. (2006, p. 246)

After the students compute the cost per bomber compared to the cost of tuition at a state university in Wisconsin, they compare these figures. Next, he has them write their opinion of this situation and then write how they feel about doing math in this way. With projects such as these, that transcend overly guarded walls between disciplines, Gutstein's work is a step in the right direction! (Gutstein, 2006, p. 247)

Verbal Thinking

None of these kinds of thinking exists in isolation. Ideally, they can all work together as they shape and are shaped by one another. In considering Vygotsky's idea of the dialectic relationship between thinking and speaking, we may be able to grasp the many ways that cognitive pluralism can help create bridges between outer to inner speech. Afterward, through personal concept formation, these diverse ways of knowing can be expressed through the medium of speaking, writing and communication of every kind. Language is communication; as such it serves as a

> bridge between individuals who wish to overcome divisions born of the diversity of human experience. It is also a bridge between inner thought and shared understanding: the past and the present, the world of the senses and the realm of thought. (John-Steiner, 1985, p. 111)

Thinking evolves as communication through speaking and writing processes on bridges between inner thought and shared understanding that John-Steiner mentions. As an example of this process she goes on to quote the playwright Arthur Miller:

> For myself it has never been possible to generate the energy to write and complete a play if I know in advance everything it signifies and all it will contain. The very impulse to write, I think, springs from an inner chaos crying for order, for meaning, and meaning must be discovered in the process of writing or the work lies dead as it is finished. (ibid., p. 133)

Miller's description of how meaning is discovered in the writing process offers rich possibilities in every genre of writing for learning. The act of writing is itself a "method of inquiry, a way of finding out about yourself and your topic." Maxine Greene places writing at the center of the learning experience when she says that it is "by writing that I often manage to name alternatives and to open myself to possibilities. This is what I think learning ought to be." Writing is a form of thinking and an extension of the reading process and there are no limits to how it can be used as a medium for learning across every content area. (Greene, 1995, p. 107; Richardson, 2003, p. 499)

Verbal facility is central to all content areas of *learning,* yet as we have stated repeatedly in this chapter, the bridge between inner thought and communication is not located on a one-way street. Multiple discourses work in both directions in both spontaneous and scientific concept formation through problem recognition, conceptual blending and problem solving by serving as entry points for personalized construction of meaning and mediums of expression in communicating with others. If this is true, then why aren't these tools used more often in schools today? In a presentation given in 1993, Michael Cole comments on some of the barri-

ers to the acquisition of written language that Vygotsky acknowledged, but specific suggestions as to how we might enable our students to break through were only mentioned briefly.

The first reason given is that "writing involves a double abstraction process." The first kind of abstraction mentioned is that written speech is the absence of "intonation and expression. Written speech lacks all the aspects of speech that are reflection in sound." There is certainly something to be said for the differences between oral and written language, but by using a wide array of expressive communication as we have been discussing, these abstractions can be transformed in learning experiences. (Cole, 1993, p. 13)

One example comes from the Met Center we mentioned in the last chapter. While students spend two days a week outside the classroom with their cooperating mentors from a wide array of actual employment settings, they are required to keep a journal of their activities and then transform their journal into formal quarterly "exhibitions; digital portfolios; narratives; and, transcripts." This process certainly expresses the role of mediated activity in combining physical movement and the senses with the tone of conversations and other features that enable release from abstraction. (Retrieved from: http://metcenter.org/the-education/evaluation/)

The process described above can happen in conjunction with breaking through another barrier to writing that Vygotsky mentioned: student motivation. Vygotsky stated that "the motives that would cause one to resort to written speech are less accessible to the child when he begins to write." This hurdle can be crossed allowing the student to write about his or her own interests and desires and life experiences in a way that engage them beyond any prescribed writing methods teaching they might receive. (Vygotsky cited in Cole, 1993, p. 13; Vygotsky, 1987d, p. 203).

What comes immediately to mind as an example of this is the true story of Erin Gruwell's classroom

in Long Beach, California, in 1992, shortly after the Rodney King beatings which led to a wave of violence, rioting and murder in gang warfare. Here she describes the value of allowing her students to write anonymously at first about their fears, desires and frustrations and hopes that comprised their daily experience in the middle of the nightmarish existence of their everyday lives.

> When one of my students exclaimed, "I feel like I live in an undeclared war zone," I realized that these young people needed to be encouraged to pick up a pen rather than a gun. Tragically, this student had lost two dozen friends to gang violence. In an attempt to connect with my class, I gave my students journals in the hopes of giving them a voice. Before long, they began to pour out their stories openly, unburdened by the anxieties associated with spelling, grammar, and grades. Journals provided a safe place to become passionate writers communicating their own histories, their own insights. As they began to write down their thoughts and feelings, motivation blossomed. Suddenly, they had a forum for self-expression, and a place where they felt valued and validated. (Gruwell, 2006, n.p.)

Neither the students nor Ms. Gruwell had any idea that their stories would end up in a book that would become number 1 on the *New York Times* best-seller list after they later refined and edited their work (ibid). Here then is another example of a dynamic blending of Vygotsky's spontaneous and scientific concept formations emerging out of the visceral and cognitive inner speech of these young lives, many of whom were the first in their families to graduate from high school and go onto college.

The last barrier to written speech mentioned by Vygotsky (and cited by Cole) is that it is "speech without an interlocutor. This creates a situation completely foreign to the conversational speech the child is accustomed to . . . it is conversation with a piece of

paper." This difficulty not only creates barriers in children but in college-level students as well. One professor who has dealt effectively with this condition and used it to great advantage in cultivating student personal voice is Sylvain Nagler, a mentor at Empire State College with whom I studied in Albany, New York. Here is the advice he gives to his students with writer's block. (Vygotsky, 1987d, p. 202)

> Write this assignment as a letter to me. Don't worry about MLA or APA right now, just tell me about what you have learned from your reading. I want to learn about these topics too. *In further personal communication he adds.* If I may I would add a more contemporary version in my instructions which is for students to use the pronoun "I" when they write as a means to make links between what is outside the assigned material, and how they can link it to their personal history and to their current life circumstances and to those of others. Using "I" I believe contributes to shaping that way of thinking and learning. (Personal communication, 10/1997 and 8/3/2011)

I am one of those students for whom this method certainly worked. During my classes with Dr. Nagler, I made significant breakthroughs in writing and subsequently I was encouraged to pursue graduate studies. This would have been almost unthinkable before this period of learning to write and writing to learn.

Vygotsky and Metaphor

There are many of aspects to Vygotsky's work that were cut short or left incomplete by his untimely death. One of the areas that he wrote comparatively little about in a specific way is metaphor. Yet it is clear that he highly valued metaphor and even wrote at one point that "all the words of psychology are metaphors taken from the spatial world." This has certainly proven to be true in the decades follow-

ing his death when we think of the many metaphors for the mind that have emerged since the computer age began. But science was not the only place where we witness Vygotsky's love of figurative language. Remember in the first chapter we mentioned that his childhood friend Dobkin spoke of his lifetime love of poetry? Also we should remember that one of the main reasons that he began his work in psychology was to study ways that art and literature could release higher levels of consciousness in people. There is also the problem of losing the richness of figurative language when Vygotsky's work is translated from Russian. Rene van der Veer states that Vygotsky's writing style is "full of figurative language, rhetoric, references to novels and plays" which have been obscured by some translators. (Vygotsky, 1997c, p. 291; van der Veer, 1987, p. 175)

Finally, Vygotsky acknowledged the need for figurative language in releasing the imagination when he saw the absence of it in his aphasia patients. "When he was asked about the meaning of the phrase 'he has golden hands' the aphasiac responded: 'it means that he knows how to melt gold.'" Vygotsky observed that the patient "was not able to understand a metaphor," which also resulted in "the disappearance of thinking in concepts the imagination also drops to zero." (Vygotsky, 1998b, p. 163)

Here are some of the metaphors that did survive the translation process. It is interesting to note that almost all of these are used in describing connections between thinking and speech. *(I realize that some of these examples are actually similes, but I use the word* metaphor *generically to describe both types of figurative language.)* "A thought may be compared to a cloud shedding a shower of words." And he metaphorically describes the formation of inner speech as "a process that involves *the evaporation of speech* in *thought.*" This is followed by one of his most famous quotes and is found as the very end of *Thought and Language.* "Consciousness is reflected in a word as the sun in a drop of water." "A word relates to consciousness as a living cell relates to a

whole organism, as an atom relates to the universe." "A word is a microcosm of human consciousness." (1986, p. 256; 1986, p. 251; 1987e, p. 252)

In an unpublished paper, Clay Beckner discusses Vygotsky's spatial metaphor of the plane. He says that "there is a recurrent image of 'two planes of speech,' in which semantics and sound-forms are partitioned into two planes as the 'meaningful and external aspects of speech.' If you have read this far into this chapter, then by now you should be familiar with the movement of these "two planes" of thought and speech and their dialectical relationship in creating and communicating meaning. Remember earlier in the chapter we quoted Vygotsky's metaphor of clothing. "The structure of speech is not simply the mirror image of the structure of thought. It cannot, therefore be placed on thought like clothes off a rack." He also uses wind as a metaphor of motivation. "To extend this analogy, we must compare the motivation of thought to the wind that puts the cloud in motion." (Beckner, 2003 ; Vygotsky quoted in Beckner, 2003, p. 18 ; Vygotsky, 2003, p. 7; Vygotsky,1987e, p. 250–251).

The fact that all of these examples relate to the relationship between thought and word gives saliency to specific ways that metaphors are created. By extending the prevailing themes of this chapter we can suggest that metaphors are created through a blending of spontaneous and scientific concepts, old thoughts with new ones, visual language with verbal images and especially kinesthetic concepts with verbal ones. In the field of education especially, it stands to reason that the most effective variety of concept creation occurs when students are able to create metaphors for content area knowledge out of their own life experiences and it also makes sense that teachers should use analogies, stories, and metaphoric language in ways that enable students to confront the "predefined world, marked off and explained by others (usually others whom they do not know, and who do not have their interests at heart." (Greene, 2001, p. 137)

What is exactly meant by metaphor? The word comes from the combination of the Greek words *meta,* which means "over," and *pherein,* "to carry." This "carrying over" describes the blending of the features of one concept to another, in a unique combination that results in a new shade of personalized meaning. Richards describes the structure of metaphor as "two thoughts of different things active together and supported by a single word, or phrase, whose meaning is a resultant of their interaction." (Hawkes, 1972, p. 1; 1936, p. 93)

Lakoff and Johnson express this interaction as much more than just the combination of the names of objects at the sentence level. Their emphasis is on the conjoined meaning of concepts within the context of lived experience when they write that "the essence of metaphor is understanding and experiencing one kind of thing in terms of another." The traditional view of metaphor is that it is a form of figurative language that is used to dress up the literal usage of words and phrases. Many still view metaphor as fanciful or not really essential to basic communication. In the last half of the 20th century, this notion has been reexamined in the fields of psychology, neuroscience, philosophy, and linguistics. From these disciplines, a growing consensus suggests that metaphor is fundamental to the process of thinking and communicating. Lakoff and Johnson go on to say that "our conceptual system is largely metaphorical." This view includes both conscious and subconscious thought expressed outwardly in words that tie concepts together into one expression. Vygotsky's views of concept formation are implicit in this view although Lakoff and Johnson do not specifically mention his work. (Lakoff & Johnson, 1980, pp. 2–3)

When we consider that one of the primary goals of Vygotsky's work in psychology was to overcome behaviorist dualism through integrating mind, emotions and body, then the connections to his work with that of Lakoff and Johnson and others that give centrality to the physical movement in concept formation become clearer and more realistic.

One thinker who is rarely mentioned, whose views of Cartesian dualism are similar to Hegel and by extension Lev Vygotsky is Giambattista Vico. His work helped to spark the Romantic Movement by influencing the poets and writers of the late 18th century. In his work called *New Science*, he states that "it is noteworthy that in all language, the greater part of the expressions relating to inanimate things is formed by metaphors from the human body and its parts and from the human senses and passions." In Vico's view, this formation of the mind through language began through metaphorical signs and gestures. Metaphor became the primary way of knowing and understanding experience in the world. Modell acknowledges the importance Vico placed on this view by saying that "metaphor was understood not as a figure of speech, a trope, but as a vital means of understanding the world." Vico's views sound remarkably like Dewey (1934), Greene (1995), and others who welcome a pluralistic epistemology through the portals of the body and mind. (Vico, 1744, p. 405; Modell, 2003, p. 15)

Nineteen years after their first book on metaphor was published, Lakoff and Johnson support Vico's work as well through their belief that our conceptual system is shaped by both our sensorimotor and cognitive experiences. Some of the examples they give include "affection is warmth." This comes from feeling warm by being held affectionately. Another one is "difficulties are burdens." This, of course, is the result of the experience of lifting heavy objects. And "knowing is seeing" comes from our experience of obtaining information through our eyes. These examples characterize the connections between body and mind and at the same time imply to us that primary metaphorical experience is the gateway to more advanced connections required in spoken and written communication. (Lakoff & Johnson, 1999, pp. 52–54)

In Vygotsky's lifetime up to the present the prevailing framework of behaviorism has had little use for metaphor because it is predicated on the belief

that all "scientific knowledge can be reduced to a system of literal and verifiable sentences." In behaviorism, only quantifiable outcomes are relevant, and while cognitive psychology acknowledges some aspects of brain lateralization, creativity, and problem solving, it rejects an emphasis on the subconscious. Even Chomsky, whose work challenged the dominance of behaviorism, still bases his work on the Cartesian split between thought and language. (Johnson, 1981, p. 17)

Just two years after Vygotsky's death in 1936, I. A. Richards published his *Philosophy of Rhetoric*, a work that grew directly out of Vico's thinking. Richards strongly challenged the literal truth paradigm through his view that metaphor is at the basis of all thought. "Thought is metaphoric, and proceeds by comparison, and the metaphors of language derive there from." In other words, he believed that at the base of all thinking, there is a metaphoric relationship. Richards takes this one step further when he suggests that metaphors are "cognitively irreducible" or cannot be reduced to statements of literal meaning. A metaphoric expression therefore becomes a newly created vehicle of meaning which loses potency when seeking to make a literal statement out of its component parts. (Richards, 1936, p. 94; Richards cited in Johnson, 1981, p. 19)

As an example of this we refer to an unpublished presentation by Akeroyd where he removed all of the metaphorical references in Frost's *The Road Not Taken*. It is hard to imagine this without metaphor, but it was something like, "I came to a fork in the road, and I took the one that had less traffic, and things worked out alright."(1986)

Literalism weakens or negates the message and blocks the multiple dimensions of rich interpretation, robbing the imagination of its greatest power as a generative interpreter of experience. Black goes so far as to say that in some cases, metaphors create new meaning rather than just offering a means of expressing old ideas in a new way. (1954/1955, pp. 273–294)

Needless to say, these ideas have not been readily welcomed by the prevailing cultures that were (and still are) dominated by positivism. Nevertheless, in the latter half of the 20th century, the power of metaphor began to take shape and branch out into philosophy, neuroscience, psychology, and education. The field of neuroscience brought about a domain of study that offered neural connections as a possible explanation to the bringing together of disparate elements in metaphor. The field of philosophy found new territory by viewing the body and mind holistically. This notion was further strengthened by feminist scholars who eschewed the objectification of the body and the dualism that exists in the Cartesian analysis of the mind as distinct from the body. Eventually, the field of education also found a measure of receptivity to the synthesis of body and mind.

Does this mean that we cannot think without metaphor? Of course the answer is no. As we discussed in the use of private speech and inner speech, there are often times when we think literally. For example we might say out loud "hungry" or "tired." There is no end to the use of thought and word in this way. If however you were to say "a tidal wave of weariness hit me this afternoon," a much more fully developed description of your condition is revealed.

Metaphor is also very important in helping us come to grips with our internal conditions in a way that assist us in ongoing identity formation and making sense of our experience. The use of metaphor in self-discovery is very evident in the work of Ming Fang He in her account of the struggle of three Chinese women teachers to find and maintain their identities in the culture of the North American academic world, as she relied heavily on the "flowing quality of the river metaphor." Because the Chinese language and culture are strongly metaphoric, she found a natural transition in using metaphor to articulate her journey of "personal and professional identity development and knowledge transformation in our acculturation and enculturation processes in China and Canada." Her writing demonstrates the

power of Heidegger's statement that "language is the house of Being." In the midst of all the outward changes in circumstances, metaphor can provide a source of an abiding personal connection to the self and the way it relates to the world and others. (He, 2003, pp. 129–130; Heidegger, 1947, p. 217)

This is made possible by the relativistic character of metaphoric language and gives credence to Vygotsky's views of the fluid nature of language as it emerges from sociocultural and sociohistorical contexts in meaning making.

Because each culture makes meaning in widely diverse ways, language forms and usage might have complex intricacies and shades of meaning on one concept alone. The standard example of this is how time is viewed differently by different cultures. (This does not include the popular myth that the Hopi tribe of Indians does not have a word for time—it is simply not true.) However there are plenty of examples from the present day that suggest ways that language can shape thought. Consider the Australian aboriginal language, Guugu Yimithirr, spoken in north Queensland, which has no words for right or left, in front of, or behind to describe location. Instead they use the points of the compass even when requesting that someone move over to make room. They will say "move a bit to the east." To tell you where exactly they left something in your house, they'll say, "I left it on the southern edge of the western table." (Deutscher, 2010, p. MM 42)

The effect on the thinking of this group is phenomenal in orienting the speakers to their directional spatial environment to such that roughly 1 out of every 10 words in conversational Guugu Yimithirr includes either north, south, east or west and is accompanied with precise hand gestures (ibid). Consequently in this culture, language acquisition involves constant awareness of spaces relative to the points of the compass. Deutscher relays a fascinating story about the ways that memory is stored for the speakers of this language. The story also serves as a clear example of Vygotsky's notion of lan-

guage as a mediating tool as a means of creating higher levels of consciousness through spatial kinesthetic approaches to meaning creation.

> One Guugu Yimithirr speaker was filmed telling his friends the story of how in his youth, he capsized in shark-infested waters. He and an older person were caught in a storm, and their boat tipped over. They both jumped into the water and managed to swim nearly three miles to the shore, only to discover that the missionary for whom they worked was far more concerned at the loss of the boat than relieved at their miraculous escape. Apart from the dramatic content, the remarkable thing about the story was that it was remembered throughout in cardinal directions: the speaker jumped into the water on the western side of the boat, his companion to the east of the boat, they saw a giant shark swimming north and so on. Perhaps the cardinal directions were just made up for the occasion? Well, quite by chance, the same person was filmed some years later telling the same story. The cardinal directions matched exactly in the two tellings. Even more remarkable were the spontaneous hand gestures that accompanied the story. For instance, the direction in which the boat rolled over was gestured in the correct geographic orientation, regardless of the direction the speaker was facing in the two films (ibid).

This story also serves as a reminder that linguistic differences should not be viewed as liabilities. Instead we should see them as assets to the entire family of humans that keep homogeneity at bay by creating spaces for multiple ways of thinking, communicating, problem solving and being in the world. The examples of people used in this chapter, Temple Grandin, Ansel Adams, Kim Peek, Albert Einstein, Helen Keller, Jason the bottle collector, Erin Gruwell and her students, Arthur Miller, and the speakers of Guugu Yimithirr are all unique treasures whose lives and work confirm to us the existence of vastly diverse ways in which thinking, speech, meaning creation and problem solving all work together in holistic unity. But this dialectical harmony does not exist statically or deterministically. Vygotsky writes at the end of *Thought and Language*, "The connection between thought and word however is neither preformed nor constant. It emerges in the course of development and itself evolves."(1986, p. 255)

A friend of mine told me that his son was weaned from the bottle in one day. He looked at the wonderful food his parents were eating, stood up in his high chair, and threw his bottle on the kitchen floor and said, "No more bottle!" Metaphorically I read this as "no more prescribed or predigested formula food!" More and more of today's students want firsthand knowledge in seeing, discovering, and understanding and making meaning through their own unique ways of thinking, conceptual blending and expressing their voice in the rich variety of human experience. It is our job as educators to create zones of proximal development that are culturally and cognitively appropriate for each of our students. Our fulfillment comes out of witnessing the ways that they appropriate, personalize and express their thought and speech in creating meaning.

Glossary

Inner Speech—refers to a unique form of inner dialogue with oneself comprised of both speech and "a distinct plane of verbal thought" which is "comprised of pure meanings." Vygotsky believed that these meanings were in an abbreviated or truncated form that cannot be literally transcribed into outer speech but require diverse means of cognitive processing in order to become meaningful communication. These may include rational, visual, somatic, musical and emotional expressions through a vast expanse of genres and discourses within the context of a given culture. (Vygotsky, 1986, pp. 248–249)

Leading Activity—is a specifically guided activity that is created for the purpose of development. For example in the famous case involving Helen Keller, her teacher Anne Sullivan used

sign language to spell w-a-t-e-r after placing Helen's hands under running water.

Mediation—using a sign, symbol, or gesture that generates higher mental processes. For Vygotsky these almost always involved the use of language. A simple example can be found in the word "hot," which means "do not touch or you will experience pain." A more developed mediatory sign, could be a parent offering their son or daughter the keys to the family car, which mediates trust and responsibility.

Mediator—Anything used in the process of mediation that, once internalized, becomes a mental tool. An example could be the alphabet song, which later helps in referencing alphabetical order.

Microgenesis—This term is used in Vygotskian studies to refer to "the unfolding of a single psychological act (for instance the act of perception), often over the course of milliseconds" (Wertsch, 1991, p. 23). This involves targeting specific areas of development such as learning language tasks or solving a specific problem.

Ontogenesis—From the Greek words "onto," which means being and "genesis," meaning origin. This is a term used by Vygotsky to describe the unfolding of individual human development as a process of both biological and social forces. When applied to the processes of thinking and speech, Vygotsky saw these two aspects as separate processes within ontogenesis, but "at a certain point, the two lines cross: thinking becomes verbal and speech intellectual." According to Vygotsky the two processes become unified "when speech and practical activity, two previously completely independent lines of development, converge." (1978, p. 24; Vygotsky, 1987b, p. 112)

Phylogenesis—This term evolved from the Greek word "phylo" meaning tribe. A term used by Vygotsky that refers to the evolution of the human family. Of course he saw this not only as a biological process but also as the product of social formation mediated through the use of language which distinguishes humans from apes whom he viewed as "slaves of the situation." (cited in Wertsch, 1991, p. 20).

Private speech—is self-directed for the purpose of self-regulation and problem solving. Private speech functions in the threshold between outward communication and the unique operations of inner speech, yet all of these aspects of language overlap.

CHAPTER FOUR

Vygotsky and Imagination

In creative imagination, the emotional and intellectual aspects of the adolescent's behavior find complex synthesis (Vygotsky, 1998b, p. 166).

If human activity were limited to reproduction of the old, then the human being would be a creature oriented only to the past and would only be able to adapt to the future to the extent that it reproduced the past. It is precisely human creative activity that makes the human being a creature oriented toward the future, creating the future and thus altering his own present. This creative activity, based on the ability of our brain to combine elements, is called imagination. (Vygotsky 1930/2004, p. 9)

Most of Vygotsky's writing on imagination and creativity occurred in the last period of his life. He wrote *Imagination and Creativity in Childhood* in 1930, *Imagination and Creativity in the Adolescent* in 1931, and

Imagination and Its Development in Childhood in 1932. What Vygotsky meant by imagination is really an extension of the ideas we discussed in the previous chapter where we explored conceptual blending and metaphor creation and John-Steiner's (1995) notion of cognitive pluralism. In this concluding chapter, we will explore the highlights of Vygotsky's thoughts about imagination and creativity in several areas: reflective-generative imagination, emotional/ **empathetic imagination** and collaborative imagination. These topics require a consideration of Vygotsky's use of a Russian word—***perezhivanie***—because an understanding of this also helps us see how Vygotsky viewed all of the above topics. In the following passage he connects perezhivanie to children's environment and their emotional experience.

Empathetic imagination is a capacity that exists between a person's thoughts and emotions that makes possible the ability to resonate with, imagine and share the life experiences of others.

Perezhivanie A Russian word that is generally but weakly translated as experience in English. In the original language it is used to describe both personal emotional and intellectual experience as well as the emotional and intellectual experience of others.

The emotional experience [*perezhivanie*] arising from any situation or from any aspect of his environment, determines what kind of influence this situation or this environment will have on the child. Therefore, it is not any of the factors themselves (if taken without the reference of the child) which determines how they will influence the future course of his development, but the same factors refracted through the prism of the child's emotional experience [*perezhivanie*]. (1994, pp. 338–339)

Vygotsky used perezhivanie as a way to connect his work on the development of higher levels of mental consciousness to emotions through play as a means to cultivate imagination and creativity. Remember in the first chapter we discussed Vygotsky's interest in the work of the acting teacher, Konstantin Stanislavski? In his work,

perezhivanie is a tool that enables actors to create characters from their own re-lived, past lived through experiences. Actors create a character by revitalizing their autobiographical emotional memories and, as emotions are aroused by physical action, it is by imitating another's, or a past self's,

physical actions, that these emotional memories are re-lived. (Ferholt, 2009, p. 3)

A fitting example of this aspect of perezhivanie is used in Chapter Two in the example of Jamie Foxx portraying the life of Ray Charles. Stanislavski's method is based on the imagination of the actor to relive emotions out of their own experience as the actors "uncover the 'subtext' of their lines in a play… every sentence that we say in real life has some kind of subtext, a thought hidden behind it." A professor of drama instruction comments on Stanislavski's meaning of subtext. (Vygotsky, 1986, p. 250)

> This subtext would not be spoken, but rather, interpreted by the actor through intonation, gesture, body posture, pauses or choices in action. Thus, through the actor's imagination, the subtext "spoke" to the audience. Stanislavski said: "Spectators come to the theatre to hear the subtext. They can read the text at home." (Sawoski, 2011, p. 9)

Further in the chapter Vygotsky gives examples of subtexts from Stanislavsky's instructions to actors that contain a short description of the motives behind the text of the play. For example, next to the line *"O, Chatsky, but I am glad that you have come,"* is written *"tries to hide her confusion"* and further next to the text *"And always so, no less, no more"* is written *"Tries to reassure Chatsky. I am not guilty of anything."* Vygotsky used all of this and similar examples to argue that to "understand another's speech, it is not sufficient to understand his words—we must understand his thought. But even that is not enough—we must also understand his motivation." (Vygotsky, 1986, p. 253)

The example used in Chapter Two by Tonya Perry provides a fitting example of how this can be used in education. After the students saw video footage of Jews being rounded up and shoved into the cattle cars of a trains bound for death camps, they were able to draw on their own experiences of fear. I am

sure for almost all of them the level of fear they had experienced held no comparison to the real lives of the Anne Frank family, but that is where imagination, emotion, movement and intellect all intersect.

Perezhivanie and Empathetic Imagination

So by using perezhivanie as our framework, we can further explore what Vygotsky wrote about imagination and creativity, starting with the outline he provides in his essay written in 1930 and retranslated and printed in 2004. He lays out his argument by saying that imagination is predicated on actual experiences in the lives of children and the richer the experience (perezhivanie) the more imagination is enabled to work.

> Thus, imagination always builds using materials supplied by reality. But the ultimate elements, from which the most fantastic images, those that are most remote from reality, are constructed, these terminal elements will always be impressions made by the real world. Now we can induce the first and most important law governing the operation of the imagination. This law may be formulated as follows: the creative activity of the imagination depends directly on the richness and variety of a person's previous experience because this experience provides the material from which the products of fantasy are constructed. The richer a person's experience, the richer is the material his imagination has access to. This is why a child has a less rich imagination than an adult, because his experience has not been as rich. If we trace the history of great works, great discoveries, then we can almost always establish that they were the result of an enormous amount of previously accumulated experience. Every act of imagination starts with this accumulation of experience. All else being equal, the richer the experience, the richer the act of imagination. (pp. 14–15)

Is it possible that we can create environments in schools where children can learn to enter into the experience of others through imagination and perezhivanie? The answer to this really brings us to the present and future state of research with Vygotsky's work and how it can be applied to bring the kind of needed changes in education itself. As we stated at the end of the first chapter, one reason for skyrocketing interest in Vygotsky's work is that many of us in the field of education are passionately seeking ways to combine the very best theories of how learning takes place with present practices that do so much more than inform, but actually bring change in thinking.

One very promising project to consider is called *The Roots of Empathy,* a curriculum that originated in Canada in 1996 and is slowly catching on several other countries. In this program a baby and mother visit a classroom once a month for the first year of the child's life. Founder Mary Gordon believes this relationship "is [the] best example of emotional attunement there is which is why I chose it as a model of empathy for children to experience." She goes on to describe what happens during the monthly sessions in a way that provides another fascinating example of Vygotsky's notion of a leading activity within the ZPD. (2010, n.p.)

> In Roots of Empathy, children become scientists who explore the inner consciousness of a baby through a curriculum led by a certified instructor, who guides them to describe what the baby is feeling and how the parent is paying attention to the baby's needs. This powerful learning is then extended outwards so children identify and reflect on their own thoughts and feelings and those of others (empathy). For many children, this is the only time where we actually attend to their emotional needs as well as their academic development. (ibid.)

There have been several mixed-method studies of the effects of this curriculum over the last ten years in an ongoing longitudinal study that shows a

decrease in aggression and an increase in emotional understanding and care. These results certainly support the idea that perezhivanie leads to a release of the imagination that can certainly increase through leading activities. One of the most dramatic stories comes from Gordon's 2009 book. (Schonert-Reichl, 2009)

Darren was the oldest child I ever saw in a Roots of Empathy class. He was in Grade 8 and had been held back twice. He was two years older than everyone else and already starting to grow a beard. I knew his story: his mother had been murdered in front of his eyes when he was four years old, and he had lived in a succession of foster homes ever since. Darren looked menacing because he wanted us to know he was tough: his head was shaved except for a ponytail at the top and he had a tattoo on the back of his head.

The instructor of the Roots of Empathy program was explaining to the class about differences in temperament that day. She invited the young mother who was visiting the class with Evan, her six-month-old baby, to share her thoughts about her baby's temperament. Joining in the discussion, the mother told the class how Evan liked to face outwards when he was in the Snugli and didn't want to cuddle into her, and how she would have preferred to have a more cuddly baby. As the class ended, the mother asked if anyone wanted to try on the Snugli, which was green and trimmed with pink brocade. To everyone's surprise, Darren offered to try it, and as the other students scrambled to get ready for lunch, he strapped it on. Then he asked if he could put Evan in. The mother was a little apprehensive, but she handed him the baby, and he put Evan in, facing towards his chest. That wise little baby snuggled right in, and Darren took him into a quiet corner and rocked back and forth with the baby in his arms for several minutes. Finally, he came back to where the mother and the Roots of Empathy instructor were waiting and he

asked: "If nobody has ever loved you, do you think you could still be a good father?" (pp. 5–6)

Through this experience (perezhivanie) Darren began to imagine himself differently and perhaps he experienced a small shift in his sense of personal agency. It would be interesting to follow up on Darren himself to see how these learning experiences may have shaped his development. Next we consider the ways that fictional or nonfictional stories can open the imagination through shared experiences. Like all areas of development in Vygotsky's work, he saw imagination as a co-constructed dynamic that emerges out of links formed in real-life experiences of identification with others. His argument is that on the surface level, it does not really matter whether the stories of others is true or not or even if one's own experience completely corresponds to the subjects of the story. Imagination, cognition and emotion all unite with our own experience in ways that create empathy and break the crusts of the predictable and the given.

> This type of linkage is made possible by virtue of the experience of someone else or so-called social experience. . . . It becomes the means by which a person's experience is broadened, because he can imagine what he has not seen, can conceptualize something from another person's narration and description of what he himself has never directly experienced. He is not limited to the narrow circle and narrow boundaries of his own experience but can venture far beyond these boundaries, assimilating, with the help of his imagination someone else's historical or social experience. In this form, imagination is a completely essential condition for almost all human mental activity. (Vygotsky, 1930/2004, p. 17)

For present and future teachers, this aspect of imagination is absolutely vital because our students learn best by example and we cannot teach what we do not practice in our own lives. Imaginative and

empathetic understanding can open up dialogue with each student in ways that are culturally responsive and mutually respectful. The following anecdotes come from my undergraduate class on Diversity in Educational Contexts and reveal the power of personal story in creating empathy. These quotes are used with their permission.

> This course has also opened my eyes to how the dominant culture dictates the direction of our curriculum. Our history is evident of this and although we look back with a bit of shame, we continue the practice of prejudice and stereotyping with the dominant culture making all the rules. I have to admit that now that I am at the completion of this class, I now have a more open mind to others around me. I noticed that just because the girl sitting next to me is the same race as me doesn't mean she feels the same way on certain topics. For instance one day our class was discussing our relationships with our parents. The girl next to me seemed to be a mama's girl that likes to be the girly girl. It turned out that she plays rugby and talks to her dad on a daily basis. (Stephanie Mincey, 2010)

Another student comments on the story of a classmate who up until recently was an "unregistered alien." She was in fact, one of my best students last year and her story touched each of us profoundly.

> What I view as the turning point was when a female student in class opened up about the Mexican *coyotes*. I had never heard this term before, and in all honesty I just assumed that people who crossed the border merely had to walk across a fence when a guard's back was turned and they were in. It was seeing the raw human struggle that changed me. All of a sudden, the term *illegal alien* was no longer some abstract concept attached to a subhuman, taco eating fiend, it was someone's mother. It was a she, and that started a change in me. (Nico Adams, 2010)

As we continue with Vygotsky's essay, we read of the process of imagination and emotion flowing in two directions, both influencing and being influenced by each other.

> While, in the example we described, emotion influences imagination, in other cases imagination influences emotion. This phenomenon could be called the law of the emotional reality of the imagination. Ribot formulates the essence of this law as follows. "All forms of creative imagination," he says, "include affective elements." This means that every construct of the imagination has an effect on our feelings, and if this construct does not in itself correspond to reality, nonetheless the feelings it evokes are real feelings, feelings a person truly experiences. The passions and fates of imaginary characters, their joys and sorrows move, disturb, and excite us, despite the fact that we know these are not real events, but rather the products of fantasy. This occurs only because the emotions that take hold of us from the artistic images on the pages of books or from the stage are completely real and we experience them truly, seriously, and deeply. (1930/ 2004, pp. 19–20)

These views were radical departures from the existing conventional wisdom of the scientific age in the early 20th century. At that time (and even up to the present) objective measures dominated education. The idea that school should have anything to do with educative subjective emotional experiences has often been considered "crackpot" or "off the deep end" in many circles. Yet it is clear that students need "emotional literacy" in some cases even more than the standard cognitive operations of language, math, and science and that creative people tend to be more adaptable and therefore better able to find their way through the human predicament. John-Steiner and Moran comment and quote from Vygotsky on this topic.

Vygotsky asserted that creative imagination is necessary for effective functioning in society. That is, people with less creative imagination cannot remove themselves from the immediate stimuli of the environment. "We saw that the zero point of imagination . . . appears in the following way—the individual is in a state where he is unable to abstract himself from a concrete situation, unable to change it creatively, to regroup signs to free one's self from under its influence." (Vygotsky 1931/1998d, p. 152) The creative imagination makes people more adept at manipulating signs and psychological tools and, therefore, at adapting to their social environments. (Moran & John-Steiner, 2003, p. 68)

Imagination, Music and the Arts

According to Vygotsky another means to release imagination is through personal emotional connections with works of art. These phenomena can be instrumental in creating seamless unity between present experience and the creation of new forms, ideas, inventions and relationships. He had this to say about these connections.

Frequently a simple combination of external impressions, such as a musical composition, induces a whole complex world of experiences and feelings in a person listening to the music. This expansion and deepening of feelings, their creative restructuring constitutes the psychological basis for the art of music. (Vygotsky, 1930/2004, p. 20)

The emotional-cognitive connections found in music have long been the source of the kinds of "creative restructuring" Vygotsky mentions here, and as such, they are able to help facilitate the development of imagination in a wide range of educational settings. One of these, of course, has to do with memory and mental imaging. Advertisers make frequent use of this by connecting music to past events connected with emotions. One recent negative example of this dynamic is a commercial for Visa that uses the Moody Blues song "Tuesday Afternoon" while images of a father and daughter at an aquarium are rolling with the voice of Morgan Freeman talking in his deity-toned voice about the "freedom" that can be experienced from using a credit card.

A magnificent example comes to us from the biography of Władysław Szpilman who hid in the Warsaw Ghetto, and later in the Aryan section, during the Jewish Holocaust. Szpilman was a classical pianist whose work before and after the war was playing on Poland's National Public Radio. His story was made into the Oscar-winning movie *The Pianist*. This excerpt is written by his son, Andrzej Szpilman.

> And as the war finally drew to a close, it was once again Szpilman's art that saved him: alone for months on end in the ruins of Warsaw, he used music to give himself strength, going through all the pieces he knew in his head. I was very close to my father, but I was never able understand where this delicate man found the superhuman strength to overcome all the dreadful things he experienced. Music seemed to me to be the only possible answer. In November 1944, at temperatures well below minus 20° centigrade, my father was close to starvation when a German officer found him in his hiding-place. The German was obviously filled with despair himself, and longed for some music in the wasteland of the ruined city. He asked my father to play the piano for him. An astonishing stroke of luck if ever there was one: the chance of coming across a German humanist in Warsaw at this time and under these circumstances was about nil. And yet the two men were united by their love of music. Hosenfeld brought my father food several times, and helped him find a better hiding-place. Only in 1950 did my father manage to find out the officer's name. Immediate attempts were made to rescue Captain Wilm Hosenfeld, but in vain: at this time, the Russians were not inter-

ested in releasing a West German soldier from their POW camps, and Wilm Hosenfeld died in Stalingrad in 1952. (Szpilman, 2005, retrieved from http://www.szpilman.net/)

After the war Szpilman created many new compositions for children and adults. He lived until July 2000 by the astonishing emotional power of music that, through the imagination, helped him stay alive. This process works through connecting past experience with the present and ideally finds its way in opening new forms. These new forms represent the difference between reproductive imagination and creative imagination. Further examples of this difference can be found in recent music history from the early life of Bob Dylan. When he first began his career, reproductive imagination was strongly at work as he emulated an earlier singer, Woody Guthrie. Dylan sang like Guthrie and even dressed like him. A few years later Dylan established himself as one of the most creative and prolific song writers in recent history and certainly exemplifies creative imagination.

However we must be careful not to treat these examples as so out of reach to all but a special class of creative people. This thought stands completely against what Vygotsky writes about the zone of proximal development and "height psychology." Each learner in our classrooms is capable of releasing the imagination in the areas for which their interests and desires draw them. Our role is to help students find out what those motivating factors might be as in the case of Darren and the Snugli in the previously mentioned

Sensing Gaps and Imagination

It is impossible to create anew without a critical aspect of imagination. Otherwise the status quo is never challenged and the ability to reject static or even false or obsolete views, ideas, products, motives and answers does not come into play. Remember that Vygotsky's entire philosophy of development is based on Hegel's views of thesis-antithesis-synthesis. In this nonlinear model of "spiral curriculum" self-reflection within the dialectic of recreating and newly creating is another source of the process of development. Mary Henle writes that creativity arises from sensing gaps that beckon inquiry. Henle enumerates several reasons that gaps are sensed in our experience. These include "contradictions of all kinds" as well as "unexpected similarities." Problem finding also arises "when we encounter strange, unusual, striking, or new phenomena." Henle also mentions "difficulties arising out of the formal characteristics of prevailing theories." For example, in Vygotsky's views of behaviorism and reflexology he sensed many of these sorts of gaps which led his views of development and all that we have covered in this book. (Henle, 1986, pp. 173–181)

How might we impart this kind of reflective thinking in our students? Can we provide them with leading activities in a ZPD for this too? The most effective way of course is by our own modeling behaviors of imagining against the grain. But this capacity also requires scaffolding in order to be internalized by those that we teach. There are excellent examples of activities for helping create critical imagination that are suggested by the Center for Media Literacy website. Through the influence of Paulo Freire's writing, the founder, Elizabeth Thoman, came up with this underlying methodology:

> Through a four-step "inquiry" process of Awareness, Analysis, Reflection, and Action, media literacy helps young people acquire an empowering set of "navigational" skills which include the ability to: Access information from a variety of sources, analyze and explore how messages are "constructed" whether print, verbal, visual or multi-media, evaluate media's explicit and implicit messages against

one's own ethical, moral and/or democratic principles. Express or create their own messages using a
variety of media tools. (pt. 1, retrieved from:
http://medialit.org/about_cml.html#edphil)

One of the best samples of the work of this group
is the presentation of *Five Key Questions That Can
Change the World*. These questions are designed to
help students develop critical imagination through
the constant exposure of media messages in adver-
tisements, commercials, websites and every form of
text. They are listed as: *Who created this message?
What creative techniques are used to attract my attention? How might different people understand this message differently than me? What values, lifestyles, and
points of view are represented in, or omitted from, this
message? Why is this message being sent?*

These same questions are broken down for young
children like this:

*What is this? How is it put together? What do I see
or hear, smell, touch or taste? What do I like or dislike
about this? What might other people think and feel
about this? What do I think and feel about this? What
does this tell me about how other people live and behave?
Is anything or anyone left out? Is this trying to tell me
something? Is this trying to sell me something?* (Share,
Jolls & Thoman, 2005, pp. 9, 12)

This simplified version still asks potent questions
and provides a foundation for getting children to
think about these kinds of issues even in elementary
schools. We certainly know that advertisers understand the power of their influence with young children. Why not equip them at the same time to
question and think on their own? Certainly this is
part of what it means to use the imagination to sense
gaps. It is out of the sense that something is missing
that creativity, through the world making power of
imagination, brings forth changes in every domain,
both public and private. In the milieu of critical consciousness, the act of creating or re-creating can begin
in childhood and extend through a whole lifetime.

Creative Collaboration

This whole section is inspired by John-Steiner's work *Creative Collaboration*. A statement on the dust jacket aptly sums up the purpose of her work and this section as well.

> Rodin's sculpture "The Thinker" dominates our collective imagination as the purest representation of human inquiry—the lone stoic thinker. But while the Western belief in individualism romanticizes this perception of the solitary creative process, the reality is that scientific and artistic forms emerge from joint thinking, passionate conversations, emotional connections, and shared struggles common in meaningful relationships. (John-Steiner, 2000, dust jacket)

One of the greatest gifts that Vygotsky's work offers to those of us involved in teacher preparation, and education in general, is his continual emphasis on collaboration in the ZPD. To most of the cultures in the world in Vygotsky's time and up the present, collaboration was and is a cultural given. It is only in Western cultures with a strong emphasis on individualism and individual achievement that creative collaboration has been less prominent. It is precisely in the areas of creative collaboration and the cultivation of learning communities that will continue to keep Vygotsky's work relevant in the next decade of the 21st century and beyond.

Once again we turn to Vygotsky's use of perezhivanie to provide us with a key to understanding his view of collaboration in creativity and imagination. Two translators of Vygotsky's work provide this insight into perezhivanie. "The Russian term serves to express the idea that one and the same objective situation may be interpreted, perceived, experienced or lived through by different children in different ways." This definition calls forth the need for creative collaboration in order to be open to see and

hear from the vantage point of difference. (van der Veer & Valsiner, 1994, p. 354)

The ability to listen to others requires imagination because, by it, we are opened to the polyphonic aspect of meaning, not just the narrow sounds of cliché or the kind of inward thoughts that cause knee-jerk reactions to what we hear. The unimaginative person is only in tune with themselves. Creative collaboration "is a matter of attunement, an auditory rather than visual conception, in which the sound of music (for Aoki, jazz specifically) being improvised is an apt example." Perezhivanie creates environments that help tune the inner ear's ability to participate and resonate with the voice of others. This is no scripted endeavor, but like the jazz analogy, there is a certain aspect of the spontaneous that is welcomed. In the shared dimensions of spontaneous dialogue, there is a fuller experience of knowing and creating anew. (Pinar, 2004, p. 189)

Sidorkin offers further insight into the dynamic of creative collaboration in his view that relations cannot be described by only one person's perspective. "Relation in general is possible only in the presence of difference. Totally identical entities cannot relate to each other. Relations result from plurality, from some tension born of difference." In other words this difference is not something that needs to be overcome by a "fifty/fifty split." Every voice needs to be heard, not lowered to the least common denominator. (Sidorkin, 2002, p. 98)

Sidorkin goes on to say that one of the greatest needs in schools is the cultivation of curriculum as conversation by focusing on the ability to "read" relationships to reflect on these cases, to talk and write about relationships. The key skill here is the ability to reconstruct the other voice. A teacher must develop this ability to hear what has not been said, to formulate what his students are not able to articulate, to engage in a dialogue when the other party may not be willing or ready to engage. The ability to understand human relations relies heavily

on the heightened ability to hear and respond without preconceived notions of truth. (p. 100)

This ability to read relationships will carry over into all content areas. In fact, our praxis becomes more relevant, and potent, to the degree that we are in tune with the voice of others. This notion covers many aspects of education because language is central to both learning and communication. Imagination can provide insight into the ways language is *perceived or received* by others.

We have only just barely opened the door on this topic of collaborative creativity. There are practices too numerous to mention that are vital to every aspect of life in the 21st century as we become more and more identified as interdependent globalized yet increasingly diverse members of the human family. As we look at the present state of education, politics, the global economy, the many varieties of philosophical and religious dogmas, the need for the cultivation of creative collaboration becomes blatantly obvious. Those of us that are responsible for preparing teachers should focus as much on teaching and modeling relational "interdependent, intellectual and emotional processes" as we do our specific content areas of knowledge. (John-Steiner, 2000, p. 196)

Glossary

Empathetic imagination—is a capacity that exists between a person's thoughts and emotions that makes possible the ability to resonate with, imagine and share the life experiences of others.

Perezhivanie—A Russian word that is generally but weakly translated as experience in English. In the original language it is used to describe both personal emotional and intellectual experience as well as the emotional and intellectual experience of others.

Vygotsky, Critical Pedagogy, and the Four Commonplaces of Curriculum

Commonplace

When used as a noun in the context of this study it is simply referring to the generally accepted features of a concept. In this case the concept is curriculum.

Coalescence

literally means to grow together in forming new living organisms.

In this concluding chapter we will explore convergence between Vygotsky's work and critical pedagogy through a framework provided by Joseph Schwab's notion of four **commonplaces**. Schwab had much to say about the social aspect of learning and the need for "discovery and invention (through) pluralities of knowledge." Some of the terminology that Schwab brought to the field of education from his background in biology is rich with metaphors of life and nature. In fact it was Schwab who referred to the field of curriculum as "moribund" by the end of the 1960s. Another potent word he brought from biology is **coalescence** "which literally means to grow together in forming new living organisms." This concept bears weighty relevance to all of Vygotsky's work as he sought for a "psychology of art" which focused on the coalescence of art and literature with studies of perception

and higher mental processes. Coalescence is an important aspect to understanding Schwab's notion of four commonplaces because, like all of Vygotsky's work, these commonplaces continually grow together in organic oneness, and like every living organism, they overlap in their function. They are only be delineated for the sake of inquiry and discussion. The four commonplaces (milieus, teacher, learner, and subject matter) are integral parts of curriculum and through them we can look deeper into the ways that Vygotsky's work converges with the field of critical pedagogy in so many ways. As we explore Vygotsky's curriculum through these commonplaces we will be able to focus on various critical pedagogical activities that are situated within each of them. (Schwab, 1978, pp. 336–335; Schwab, 1969, p. 1; Vygotsky, 1925/1971; Kincheloe, 2008; Malott, 2011; Trueba, 1999)

Milieus in Vygotsky's Curriculum

Schwab used the term "milieus" to describe the context of learning that included school and classroom environment, community and family, class and ethnicity, as well as values and attitudes that in the learner's environment comprise the "cultural climate." Current curriculum milieus that characterize a curriculum of standardized practices tend to be dehumanizing, abstract, and impersonal, with a focus on individual achievement, singular interpretation, and predefined answers while operating in a downward configuration of authority. (1978, pp. 366–367)

In contrast to these current curriculum milieus, Vygotsky's curricular practices are comprised of a number of elements that work together to create the environment of problem posing, personal discovery, and co-construction of knowledge that are central to understanding the purpose and function of learning in the zone of proximal development. The most vital elements in this commonplace are the dynamic of hope, critical consciousness, and the sense of belonging and care. When speaking of this kind of hope we are referring to so much more than ungrounded optimism. Hope exists by choice, and in an educative and personal dimension it finds release in refusing static representation and given knowledge, while reaching out toward that which is not yet expressed or experienced or created. Hope looks past barriers to learning, labels, and test scores and takes us out of abstraction, into humanizing and personal knowledge of the entire domain of education, society, and culture. Vygotsky's vistas of hope are referred to earlier in this book in terms such as height psychology which "views the heights of potentiality of the individual, also including unconscious components; and, the unconscious is viewed as the seat of creativity and problem solving." In addition to a humanistic view of individuals, Vygotsky's pursuit for a new method in psychology was rooted in a quest for a new kind of collective humanity that would break free of enslavement and exploitation and transform the natural world rather than being a slave to biological forces. Once this is underway, he reasoned, there "will come the liberations of the human personality from its fetters which curb its development." And further, he adds that "new forms of labor create the new man." (Robbins, 2011, p. 19; Vygotsky, 1994, pps. 181–183)

So Vygotsky's hope was predicated on a view of transformative social, intellectual and labor activities that had the potential to create higher levels of consciousness, and this perception influenced all of his ideas about pedagogy as well. This kind of hope is one of many areas of vital convergence between Vygotsky and Freire. As we consider the hardships they both endured, it is clear that the idea of hope was not just a theory. In Vygotsky's case, just recall the events we discussed in Chapter One. In Freire's case, in 1994, after having suffered so much misunderstanding and injustice, including living in exile, he wrote:

> Without hope there is little we can do. It will be hard to struggle on, and when we fight as hopeless or despairing persons, our struggle will be suicidal. We shall be beside ourselves, drop our weapons, and throw ourselves into sheer hand-to-hand, purely vindictive, combat. (p. 9)

I have been amazed at the number of people in the field of education who have ceased to reach beyond, either because they were tired of fighting the system, or had seen too much, and had given in to despair. This is especially true with many critical educators who can very clearly name the obstacles and discern root cause and effect of oppression but they are unable to imagine or practically work to the creation of new order in place of the old.

Neither Vygotsky nor Freire would ever separate hope from critical thinking or problem posing/solving education because in their respective curricular and pedagogical milieus, hope and agency increase when knowledge is constructed through process and not just as an end in itself. Indeed for Vygotsky, "the activity of producing was inseparable from the product." (Newman & Holtzman, 1993, p. 74)

In Vygotsky's milieu there is a constant activity of critical and creative thinking, concept formation and reflection that leads to internalization and outward expression. These features are not necessarily linear as in a smoothly executed five-step lesson plan. A process of this variety may go in and out and up and down the way life itself exists within relationships of proximal development. This kind of milieu is never just a "setting...or a scene...or a series or scenes...life if you will is seamless, continuous performance." (ibid) In Vygotsky's milieu there is a seamless continuity between school and life.

Freire's notion of critical consciousness is convergent with Vygotsky in this kind of milieu and again it should be thought of as more of a continually active process of thought "that links the creation of critical citizens to the development of a radical democracy." As such it inspires students more about how to inquire, rather than provide answers in isolated and decontextualized ways to questions that students are not asking. In short, one of the primary goals of Vygotsky's curricular milieu is the nurturing and sustaining of a spirit of quest. (Aronowitz & Giroux, 1991, p. 188)

Another vital element in Vygotsky's curricular milieu that is often excluded in the scholarship about his work is the presence of interpersonal care. As we discussed in the last chapter Vygotsky's view of the role of emotions in learning has only recently gotten serious attention in the field of cognitive sciences. Yet here is what he had to say about it.

> The separation of the intellectual side of our consciousness from its affective, volitional side is one of the fundamental flaws of all of traditional psychology. Because of it thinking is inevitably transformed into an autonomous flow of thoughts thinking themselves. It is separated from all the fullness of real life, from the living motives, interests, and attractions of the thinking human. (Vygotsky, cited in Wertsch, 1985, p. 189; Goldstein, 1999)

The milieu of the zone of proximal development is one of interpersonal connection and cooperation, and as such, it is only natural to include an emphasis on the ethic of care as described by Nel Noddings when she says that "I take on the other's reality as possibility and begin to feel its reality. I feel also, that I must act accordingly; that is, I am impelled to act as though in my own behalf, but in the behalf of the other." This is very similar to Freire's notion of the other as "subject" rather than "object" which requires a relationship of trust, one of true solidarity which "requires that one enter into the situation of those with whom one is solidary." Students are quite adept at distinguishing the difference between patronization and solidarity and the distinction is only overcome by a sense of care, belonging, and heartfelt safety of a sense of self. (Noddings, 1984, p. 30; Freire, 1970, p. 49)

One of the expressions of care Noddings mentions is the "act of affirming and encouraging the best in others." This goes beyond the rote use of phrases like "good job" or any other non critical use of cliché. The act of affirming is the very practice of height psychology, expressing hope and seeing students as subjects. Jaime Escalante was masterful at creating this milieu with Latino students in East Los Angeles in the 1980s and early 1990s in his calculus classes. (1998, p. 192)

One of Escalante's former students was quoted in a wonderful interview for National Public Radio.

> Everything we are, we owe to him, says Sandra Munoz, an attorney who specializes in workers' rights and immigration cases in East Los Angeles. She was not originally an Escalante student. But that's what he'd do, she says. He'd see someone and decide they needed to be in his class. So he pulled me out my sophomore year and put me in his class, and I took math with him. He would teach anybody who wanted to learn—they didn't have to be designated gifted and talented by the school. (Munoz, cited in Bates, 2010)

Escalante was able to see potential in his students that went beyond the "barrio kids" label. The milieu of the neighborhood that his school was situated in was one of poverty, and multiple barriers to higher education, the exact opposite of a hopeful and caring environment. But both Vygotsky and the school of critical pedagogy give primacy to action which transforms negative natural environments and those that live in them through collective activities that raise self-expectation and personal agency through zones of proximal development that are imbued with these aspects of milieu. When every voice is welcomed and personal meaning is treasured, when the art of imaginative listening is continually cultivated and difference is seen as strength, not weakness, the sense of belonging and personal care will certainly flourish. In this milieu, critical consciousness and questioning will become more effective because learners will be less likely to be cynical in an environment of hope. By the same token, hope can become more substantial when static knowledge and cliché, stereotype and insincerity are brought to light by critical questioning.

The Commonplace of Teaching

The commonplace of the teacher in Vygotsky's curriculum converges well with the most widely known features of critical pedagogy. For example, the use of dialogical engagement and the co-construction of knowledge instead of the traditional view of the banking model of education wherein the teacher acts and the students passively receive are two of the most salient features.

A central feature of critical pedagogy is the notion of praxis. "Here, *praxis* denotes the moments of real human activity that occur only once (Bakhtin, 1993), which distinguishes it from the notion of practice, which is used to denote a patterned form of action, inherently a theoretical signified." (Roth & Lee, 2007, p. 190)

In other words in praxis, there are no rote teaching practices that lack critical reflection and considerations of personal socio-cultural context. Still the emphasis in praxis is active engagement. The teacher's role in this process is understood in facilitating the personal construction of meaning in the student. Think back to the example in Chapter two of a driver's training instructor with a separate steering wheel, accelerator and brake. The teacher facilitates driving instruction, but if he or she dominates the process by applying the brake or gas pedal too often, the student driver may become too passive and compliant and never learn to drive. As a facilitator, the teacher or mentor creates opportunities for activity-based learning and maximizes the release of internalization and externalized activity. The following story of an environmental project in

Western Canada provides an excellent example of the role of a teacher in Vygotskian critical pedagogy.

One day, the two co-teachers of a seventh-grade class brought a newspaper article describing the efforts of an environmental group concerned with the health of the local watershed in which the village lies and its major water-carrying body, Henderson Creek. Besides a plea for improving the sorry state of the polluted creek, the article called for a better understanding of the ecosystem as a whole. The teachers asked the students whether they were interested in doing something about it. Excited by the challenge, the students immediately began to brainstorm what they could do, including cleaning up and documenting the litter that had been discarded there. To help students in framing viable projects, the teachers organized an exploratory field trip, assisted by parents and environmentalists, and then brought the children to different spots along the creek. Mediated by teacher questions and inspired by visiting environmentalists, biologists, water technicians, First Nations elders, and local residents, the students, in groups of three to four individuals, then designed their own projects that concretely realized the general call of the environmentalists to generate scientific knowledge and to rescue the creek . The students enjoyed relative freedom over the design and implementation of their studies. For example, one group of four girls decided to take photographs at various places along the creek and to record their descriptions and impressions on audiotape. Another group decided to sample the creek at different locations for microorganisms and to correlate their frequencies with water velocity. Yet another group decided to investigate stream profiles and to correlate stream speed with depth, while the last group planned to document and identify all plants that grew in the immediate vicinity. Every other week, the class dispersed for an entire afternoon, with parents acting as drivers who brought student groups to project sites and assisted in supervision.

Some parents also worked alongside the children after having received instruction from the teachers in asking productive rather than yes-no questions. During school-based lessons, the children analyzed their data, engaged in discussions, or worked on a problem that one group had experienced, which with the mediation of the teachers, became a common topic for the entire class. Eventually, the students prepared for an open-house event organized by the environmentalist group at which they presented posters and mounted stations where visitors could use microscopes, dissolved-oxygen meters, or colorimeters (for determining turbidity). Many visitors, young and old, attended the open house which the environmentalists later attributed in part to the children, who incited their parents and other close relatives to attend. The local newspaper featured a story about the children's efforts, emphasizing their contributions to community-relevant knowledge, while a Web site that featured some of the children's scientific findings was created. In this unit, even students who often do not "succeed" in school science became core participants in the activity, including girls, aboriginal children, and students marginalized because of a "learning-disabled" classification. One such person was Davie, diagnosed as suffering from attention deficit hyperactive disorder (ADHD); he was regularly taken away from normal class work to receive special attention. Video recordings show that in his mathematics lessons, for example, he behaved in ways that teachers immediately labeled as problematic: He was "on task" for only a fraction of the time allotted and did not produce the requisite graphs that the teacher wanted. In the environmental unit, however, he not only generated usable data and graphs but also became a presenter in other classes, taught the teachers of other classes about how to conduct scientific inquiry in the creek, accompanied other students as a peer tutor in their biweekly fieldwork, and was an irreplaceable participant in the open

house, teaching adults and children alike about doing environmental research. Hence, who was deemed knowledgeable appeared to depend more on their involvement within specific settings rather than being an innate or stable characteristic of individuals. (Roth & Lee, 2007, pp. 192–194)

So in this case, the teachers introduced the topic in a way that drew the students in and then through the mediation of language in the form of questions, the students were initiated into problem posing based on their own interests in specific aspects of the project. The teacher's work was not complete until the students shared their own stories and experiences in their own words in producing and sharing their own work with others during the open house.

A teacher in this commonplace is also an "improvisational" artist who has the flexibility to work spontaneously and yet deliberately toward the opening of creative vision and expression in learners. In this role, the teacher functions continually in the tension between spontaneous and deliberate activity in the co-creation of personalized meaning and self-expression and, at the same time, challenges the learner to greater quality through appropriate criticism. Individual care and concern and an awareness of the process of organic time in the learner is of primary concern. By this, I am not referring to generalized categories of lifespan developmental psychology. This knowledge is more intuitive than information derived from a collection of pathologies that are applied in an objective way. Vygotsky's pedagogy is based rather on students functioning "a head taller" than the actual state of physical development. "Play creates a zone of proximal development of the child. In play a child always behaves beyond his average age, above his daily behavior; in play it is as though he were a head taller than himself." Through the example of the teacher, the student is also encouraged to become an improvisational artist in unlimited expressions of creativity in play and in work. Vygotsky's view of

the social aspect of learning necessitates a relationship between the teacher and the learner wherein both teacher and learner exercise reflective, critical, and generative imagination to discover, express, and evaluate desired learning. (Bateson,1990, p. 3; Vygotsky, 1986, p. 102)

Another important aspect of this commonplace is teaching by example and Vygotsky clearly modeled this right up until his death. If the teacher expects the learner be a passionate inquirer, he or she must also express the demeanor of always being onto something new, never static or dogmatic, but open and aware that growth is the only sign of life. This inward vitality will come through even when the teacher performs the "traditional" roles of classroom discussion on the forms that comprise the foundation for further inquiry. This could be anything from punctuation to the best way to prepare pie crusts.

Thus a teacher in Vygotskian critical pedagogy is a learner, improvisational artist, and a model of what is taught. Vygotskian education is always dialogical and the participants all have something added to their understanding. As an improvisational artist, the teacher helps create personalized meaning and self-expression in the learner through personal concern and care along with intuitive sense of timing and understanding of the learner potential. This requires both the creative and critical aspects of imagination in every encounter with the student. You cannot give what you do not have yourself. In Vygotsky's pedagogy, teachers model critical questioning and refuse static meaning and dead metaphors by actively engaging in a passionate pursuit of understanding by appreciating that learning is a process that is continually ongoing and never complete.

Subject Matter in Vygotsky's Pedagogy

As we explore this commonplace, we use Vygotsky's dialectical method by contrasting his notion of sub-

ject matter with standardized and static knowledge. For example, the lack of engagement that is present when the subject matter is presented in isolated and decontextualized units as a product of the canon of what Michael Apple calls "official knowledge"(1993) is in dialectical opposition to Vygotsky's view of knowledge as personal and holistic, not a product but a process. Standardized subject matter is often enforced on passive recipients that have learned to play the game in order to get a good grade, or by the same token, to those who despair because their real strengths are not measured by tests of standardized subject matter. This condition has been further exacerbated by "accountability" requirements from both federal and state legislation in the form of "benchmarks" in the No Child Left Behind Act of 2003. The current plan to make NCLB more "flexible" is really a major step in the wrong direction. Neil explains:

> This plan will push states into adopting highly flawed and inaccurate uses of student test scores to judge teachers and principals. In these ways, the Administration is perpetuating the very same discredited policies that have so damaged American education. These policies will continue the pressure to narrow the curriculum and teach to multiple-choice tests—pressures that have caused the recent explosion of cheating scandals. The dangers in this scheme outweigh the benefits to states of no longer having to meet unattainable—"adequate yearly progress" goals. (Neil, 2011, p. 1)

This curriculum is prescriptive and limiting rather than descriptive and narrative of actual lived experience. Also, the subject matter of a standardized curriculum is comprised of objective facts and skills that are often detached from real-life contexts by rote and mechanistic imitation. Often this is accomplished through means of verbal learning alone.

Contrast this with the above example where the entire environment of the creek was the subject matter along with "photographs, verbal descrip-

tions ... habitat characteristics (stream speed) and organisms (frequencies) using floating objects, tape measures, stop watches, and D-shaped nets." (Roth and Lee, 2007, p. 194)

In this commonplace the subject matter is boundless and multidimensional, yet holistic and personal. It is not contained in any one discipline but shuns fragmentation. It welcomes multiple meanings and newly created metaphoric connections. The only limitations on its scope are not in the subject but in the desire of the learner to reach beyond her present level of understanding through the imagination. So the subject matter can be anything from the microcosm or subatomic dimension to the macrocosm, so many light years away that even the most powerful telescope on earth cannot detect its presence because any light that may be present is still so distant that it is out of the range of measurement. In Vygotskian critical pedagogy, the whole world is a text!

In the actual experience of this, the dichotomy between objective and subjective understanding disappears. This happens when the subject matter is acquired through Vygotsky's notion of concept formation (see Chapter Three) which blends the old with the new, lived experience with the inexperienced, and the emotions along with mental faculties. It is through these connections that subject matter becomes personal as well as social.

The subject matter in Vygotsky's view welcomes polyphonic expression and dialogue across differences because the exact same subject matter could have a range of meanings to individual learners. The focus of learning can be on anything that the inquirer can question or wonder about. In fact, the subject matter often makes itself known through questions that arise out of sensed gaps from within or found problems. Also the subject matter can become multidimensional through repeated musings until new connections are made and new applications are discovered. Again Vygotsky viewed pedagogy as process not product.

Subject matter of this kind can be holistically explored across multiple content areas. For example, in his early undergraduate career my son William wrote a paper for a math class about the use of algebraic computation in the computer programming language that is needed to create video games. He also is also learning music composition through the soundtrack of video games. History, writing and science have also all been successfully taught through video games in an environment. Gee summarizes this medium of learning.

1. Games are based not on content, but on problems to solve. The content of a game (what it is "about") exists to serve problem solving.
2. Games can lead to more than thinking like a designer; they can lead to designing, since players can "mod" many games, i.e., use software that comes with the game to modify it or redesign it.
3. Gamers co-author the games they play by the choices they make and how they choose to solve problems, since what they do can affect the course and sometimes the outcome of the game.
4. Games are most often played socially and involve collaboration and competition. (2011, p. 1)

These gaming features align well with Vygotsky's view of subject matter including problem solving, fashioning new products, choosing to act instead of passively being acted upon, and finally co-constructing subject matter through collaboration, healthy competition and socialized learning.

Commonplace of the Learner

The learner in Vygotsky's pedagogy is best exemplified by his own personal history of intellectual curiosity and self-discovery. For example in Chapter One, we mentioned that Vygotsky and his friends would take on the roles of famous historical figures through role playing and act out the text of their lives. Also Vygotsky's love for literature and the arts led him into a quest to understand the role that psychology played in understanding the creative process. Remember also that Vygotsky was a thorough practitioner of collaborative learning with colleagues from childhood to the famous troika in his later years. Vygotsky always viewed the learner's role as active, participatory and fully engaged in personalized construction of knowledge. Vygotsky's continual personal quest for understanding reminds us once again of Freire's description of critical learners.

> The Learners maintain alive the flame of resistance that sharpens their curiosity and stimulates their capacity for risk, for adventure so as to immunize themselves against the banking system (of education, parenthesis, mine). In this sense, the creative force of the learning process, which encompasses comparison, repetition, observation, indomitable doubt, and curiosity not easily satisfied, overcomes the negative effects of the false teaching. (Freire, 1998, p. 32)

At this point the best example I have to further convey the role of the learner in Vygotsky's pedagogy is to share some scenes from my own educational experience. My progress in formal education as a child and adolescent was far from being illustrious. Almost all of the breakthroughs of discovery or accomplishment I can recall occurred outside of the classroom. Music has played such an important role in my journey as a learner, and yet one of the three D's I received in kindergarten was in music class.

I grew up in a working-class home of very humble means in a large family that loved to sing and play the kind of music that could best be described as Americana and classic rock. Music certainly was a prominent facet of my zone of early experiences of

proximal development. When I was around 9 years old, I remember bringing two spoons to a room in our basement where all of the empty canning jars were kept. I would tap each jar with a spoon to hear the tone each one created and add or remove water to tune each one and then line them up to play simple songs. Of course, I was not aware of all that I was learning about sound waves and scales, nor was I aware of the foundation that this form of play as inquiry was giving me for other aspects of learning and creativity. In retrospect I am able to apply all these experiences to Vygotsky's ideas of curriculum. This can be summed up by Dewey's notion that the learner is not made for the curriculum but the curriculum is constructed for the learner. (Dewey, 1902)

The experience with the canning jars helped me to teach myself how to play the blues harmonica. There is so much about this genre of music that is intuitive. I remember reading a few sentences of "method" on the paper insert enclosed in my newly purchased instrument, but learning to play fits Vygotsky's idea of imitation, internalization and externalized expression. First of all, I learned to reflect the sounds I heard others playing and then generate my own signature sounds. This experience led me directly to the internal dimension of learning. I had already taught myself the basics of the guitar, so when I was asked to join a band and play the harmonica, I became a guitar intern as well. I learned quite a bit by observation, as well as direct instruction from the lead guitar player. Playing in a garage band was truly one of the most productive experiences of the value in the zone of proximal development that I could have ever imagined. Out of that experience, I came to understand Vygotsky's emphasis on the role of tool and sign (in my case music) in the release of higher levels of consciousness and agency in personal development. This was followed by the externalized expression that opened spaces for my own emphasis or personal slant from a combination of technique and the very personal domain of the emotions.

At the same time that I was having such a struggle as a high school student, outside of school, I began to flourish as a musician. One strongly defining moment took place in my second year of high school. I remember hearing a song by the Lovin' Spoonful (1965) featuring a harmonica solo by John Sebastian called "Night Owl Blues." I was so drawn in by the emotional tone and skill expressed in that song that I said to myself, "I will learn to play just like that!" A few months later, I could play most of it! Not long after that, I was asked to play in a band. My level of self-confidence was altered considerably.

Fast forward through several garage bands and later accompanying myself on the guitar, to the time I met my wife Elizabeth. She once confessed that she married me "because I was nice and played the guitar." On several occasions we lived with her parents. Her father was a lawyer and her mother was an art teacher and their home was rich with academic language and books. By daily interaction in this zone of proximal development, I found myself thinking, speaking, reading and writing much more expansively in ways that brought positive changes in my view of myself as a person and life partner, as well as a father and teacher. All of these experiences have enabled me to recognize their features in all learners in one degree or another.

Vygotsky's Pedagogy Is Never Final

Through these four commonplaces there is a living configuration of pedagogy that is both theoretical and practical. At the same time, I acknowledge that Vygotsky's theories can never be captured and turned into an exact technique. Vygotsky's work is not an a priori form to be mass produced with singular specifications; it is constantly created through engaging and participatory discovery.

Vygotsky's emphasis on the role of cultural-historical context in learning conveys the idea that life is constantly changing and being changed by the

environment of social, political, and natural movement, through forces of transformative action. To Vygotsky all of life (including education) must continually renew itself through continual creative reflection and therefore it is always in the making. The element that unites all of the four commonplaces in holistic critical mass is the principle of life itself, active and dynamically present within each commonplace that creates a condition out of which personal meaning is continually created *from within* the participants.

There can be no finalized and completed form of Vygotsky's pedagogy. This is why sensing gaps, raising questions, challenging the given and the static are such important concepts. In the environment of ongoing inquiry, constant innovation and critical appraisal, there is life, and where there is life, Vygotsky's concept of education as a process is at work connecting the known with the newly discovered.

Epilogue

Vygotsky's work was a hundred years ahead of his time and brings to mind a metaphor that comes from the largest and oldest trees on the planet, the sequoia. These trees produce seeds in a cone that do not proliferate at the moment of maturity but are retained until the most advantageous environment for germination arises. This occurs after a fire when all the competing growth on the forest floor has been consumed in the heat. At that moment, the heat opens and releases the seeds of the sequoia. The present conditions in education are indeed "heating up" considerably, but the heat can also create the environment for the dissemination of Vygotsky's work that has the potential to release phenomenal development and innovation that raises learning far beyond benchmarks of standardization. If, as Michael Oakeshott suggests, that human progress is a conversation "begun in the primeval forests and extended and made more articulate in the course of centuries"

(1962, p. 490) then any serious dialogue about present and future educational reform that takes place at any level from the grassroots upward needs to include Vygotsky's voice.

Glossary

Coalescence—literally means to grow together in forming new living organisms.

Commonplace—When used as a noun in the context of this study it is simply referring to the generally accepted features of a concept. In this case the concept is curriculum.

References and Resources for Vygotskian Practice

Akeroyd, R. (1986). *The word.* (unpublished presentation). Louisville, KY.

Apple, M. (1993). *Official knowledge: Democratic education in a conservative age.* New York: Routledge.

Arnold, R. (2005). *Empathetic intelligence: Teaching, learning, relating.* Sydney: University of South Wales Press Ltd.

Aronowitz, S. and Giroux, H.A. (1991). *Postmodern education.* Minneapolis: University of Minnesota Press.

Bates, K.G. (2010). "Students 'stand and deliver' for former teacher." Retrieved from: http://www.npr.org/templates/story/story.php?storyId=124491340&ps=rs

Bateson. C. (1990). *Composing a life.* New York. The Penguin Group.

Beckner, C. (2003). *Thinking about thinking: Dialectic versus static metaphors for the mind.* Unpublished manuscript. Albuquerque: The University of New Mexico. Spring Semester.

Benjamin, S. (Producer), &. Hakford, T. (Director). (2004). *Ray* [Motion picture]. USA: Universal Studios.

Berk, L. (1992). Children's private speech: An overview of theory and the status of research. In R.M. Diaz & L. Berk (Eds.), *Private speech:*

From social interaction to self-regulation. Mahwah, NJ: Lawrence Erlbaum Associates.

Berk, L. (2004). *Awakening children's minds: How parents and teachers can make a difference.* Cary, NC: Oxford University Press.

Black, M. (1954/55) Metaphor, *Proceedings of the Aristotelian Society,* 55, 273–294.

Blanck, G. (1990). Vygotsky: The man and his cause. In: L. Moll (Ed.). *Vygotsky and Education.* New York: Cambridge University Press.

Blunden, A. (2010). *An interdisciplinary theory of activity.* Boston, MA: Brill.

Bodrova, E. & Leong, D. (1996). *Tools of the mind: The Vygotskian approach to early childhood education.* Englewood Cliffs, NJ: Prentice-Hall, Inc.

Bruner, J. (1977) *The Process of Education,* Cambridge, MA: Harvard University Press.

Cole, M. (1993).Vygotsky and writing: *Reflections from a distant discipline.* Paper presented at the 1993 Annual Meeting of the Conference on College Composition and Communication. San Diego, CA. March 31–April 3, 1993. Retrieved from: http://www.eric.ed.gov/ERICWebPortal/search/detailmini.jsp?_nfpb=true&_&ERICExtSearch_SearchValue_0=ED360627&ERICExtSearch_SearchType_0=no&accno=ED360627

Cole, M. (1996). *Cultural psychology: A once and future discipline.* Cambridge, MA: Harvard University Press.

Cole, M., & Cole, S. (Eds.) (1979) *The making of mind: The autobiography of A.R. Luria.* (pp. 189–225). Cambridge, MA: Harvard University Press.

Connery, M. C., John-Steiner, V. P., & Marjanovic-Shane, A. (Eds.) (2010). *Vygotsky and creativity: A cultural-historical approach to play, meaning making, and the arts.* New York, NY: Peter Lang.

Coreil, C. (2007). Harnessing the imagination to the neglected ear. In C. Coreil (ed.). *Imagination, cognition & language acquisition.* Jersey City, NJ: New Jersey City University Press.

Daniels, H. (Ed.) (1993). *Charting the agenda: Educational activity after Vygotsky.* London: Routledge.

Daniels, H. (Ed.) (1996). *An introduction to Vygotsky.* London: Routledge.

Daniels, H., Cole, M., Wertsch, J. V. (Eds.) (2007). *The Cambridge companion to Vygotsky.* New York, NY: Cambridge University Press.

Delpit, L. (1995). I just want to be myself: Discovering what students bring to school "in their blood." In W. Ayers (Ed.) *To become a teacher: Making a difference in children's lives.* New York: Teachers College Press.

Deutscher, G. (2010, August 29) Does your language shape how you think? *The New York Times Sunday Magazine*, p. MM 42.

Dewey, J. (1899/1956). *The child and the curriculum and the school and society*. Chicago: Phoenix.

Dewey, J. (1902). *The child and the curriculum*. Chicago, IL. University of Chicago Press.

Dewey, J. (1910/1933). *How we think: A restatement of the relation of reflective thinking to the educative process*. Boston: D.C. Heath.

Dewey, J. (1934). *Art as experience*. New York: Perigee Books.

Diaz, R. M. & Berk, L. E. (Eds.) (1992). *Private speech: From social interaction to self-regulation*. Hillsdale, NJ: Lawrence Erlbaum Associates.

Dobkin, S. (1982). Ages and days: (Semyon Dobkin's reminiscences). In Levitan, K. and Davydov, V. (Eds.), *One is not born a personality: Profiles of Soviet educational psychologists*. (pp. 11–20). Moscow: Progress Publishers.

Eisner, E. W. (1985). *The art of educational evaluation: a personal view*. London: Falmer Press.

Eisner, E. W. (1998). *The enlightened eye: qualitative inquiry and the enhancement of educational practice*. New York: Macmillan.

Emmorey, K., & McCullough, S. (2009). The bimodal bilingual brain: Effects of sign language experience. *Brain & Language, 109*, 124–132.

Ferholt, B. (2009) *The development of cognition, emotion, imagination and creativity as made visible through adult-child joint play: Perezhivanie through playworlds*. (Unpublished doctoral dissertation) University of California. San Diego, CA.

Freire, P. (1970/2003). *Pedagogy of the oppressed*. New York. Continuum.

Freire, P. (1994). *Pedagogy of hope*. Reliving pedagogy of the oppressed, New York: Continuum.

Freire, P. (1998). *Pedagogy of freedom: Ethics, democracy, and civic courage*. Lanham, MD. Rowman and Littlefield.

Freire, P., & Macedo, D. (1987). *Literacy: Reading the word and the world*. Westport, CT: Bergin & Garvey.

Gaardner, J. (1996). *Sophie's world: A novel about the history of philosophy*. New York: Berkley Publishing Group.

Gallas, K. (2003). *Imagination and literacy: A teacher's search for the heart of learning*. New York, NY: Teachers College Press.

Gee, J. P. (2011). *Ten truths about books and what they have to do with video games*. Retrieved from: http://www.jamespaulgee.com/

Goddard, H.H. (1920). *Human efficiency and levels of intelligence*. Princeton, NJ: Princeton University Press.

Goldstein, L.S. (1999). The relational zone: The role of caring relationships in the co-construction of mind. *American Educational Research Journal, 36 (3),* 647–673. Retrieved from http://www.jstor.org/stable/116553.

Gordon, M. (2009). *The roots of empathy: Changing the world child by child.* New York: The Experiment Publishers.

Gordon, M. (2010, Feb. 18). "'Empathic Civilization': Building A New World One Child At A Time." *Huffington Post.* Retrieved from: http://www.huffingtonpost.com/mary-gordon/empathic-civilization-bui_b_464359.html

Grandin, T. (2006). *Thinking in pictures, Expanded Edition: My life with autism.* New York, NY: Vintage Books.

Gray, A. (producer) & Huszar, J. (director) (1989). *Ansel Adams: Photographer.* (VHS). Beverly Hills, CA. Pacific Arts Video.

Greene, M. (1995). *Releasing the imagination.* San Francisco: Jossey-Bass.

Greene, M. (2001). *Variations on a blue guitar.* New York: Teachers College Press.

Gredler, M. E., & Shields, C. C. (2008). *Vygotsky's legacy: A foundation for research and practice.* New York, NY: The Guilford Press.

Gruwell, E. (2006). *A teacher's vision.* Long Beach, CA: Freedom Writers Foundation. Retrieved from: http://www.freedomwriters-foundation.org/site/c.kqIXL2PFJtH/b.2286935/k.92DC/A_Teachers_Vision.htm

Gutstein, E. (2006). *Reading and writing the world with mathematics: Toward pedagogy for social justice.* New York: Routledge Falmer.

Hadamard, J. (1945). *The mathematician's mind: The psychology of invention in the mathematical field.* Princeton, NJ. Princeton University Press.

Hawkes, T. (1972). *Metaphor.* London: Methuen & Co. Ltd.

He, M.F. (2003). *A River forever flowing: Cross-cultural lives and identities in the multicultural landscape.* Greenwich, CT: Information Age Publishing.

Heidegger, M. (1947). *Basic Writings.* (D.F. Krell, Ed.). New York. Harper & Row.

Heidegger, M. (1978). Letter on Humanism. In D. F. Krell (Ed.). *Basic Writings.* (p. 202). London: Routledge & Kegan.

Henle, M. (1986). *1879 and all that: Essays in the theory and history of psychology.* New York: Columbia University Press.

Hestor, M. (1967). *The meaning of poetic metaphor.* Paris: Moulton & Co.

Holzman, L. (2009). *Vygotsky at work and play.* New York, NY: Routledge.

Igoa, C. (1995). *The inner world of the immigrant child*. Mahwah, NJ: Erlbaum.

John-Steiner, V. (1985). *Notebooks of the Mind: Explorations of thinking*. New York: Harper & Row.

John-Steiner, V. (1995). Cognitive pluralism: A sociocultural approach. *Mind, Culture, and Activity,* Winter 2, (1), 2–11.

John-Steiner, V. (1997). *Notebooks of the mind: Explorations of thinking*. New York: Oxford University Press.

John-Steiner, V. (2000). *Creative collaboration*. New York: Oxford University Press.

John-Steiner, V. (2007). "Vygotsky on thinking and speaking." In H. Daniels, M. Cole, and J. Wertsch (Eds.), *The Cambridge Companion to Vygotsky* (pp. 136–154). New York: Cambridge University Press.

Johnson, J. (1994). Intra- and extrapersonal spoken language. In D. Vocate (ed.) *Intrapersonal communication: Different voices, different minds*. Hillsdale, NJ: Lawrence Erlbaum.

Johnson, M. (1981). *Philosophical perspectives on metaphor*. Minneapolis: University of Minnesota Press.

Keller, H. (1903). *The story of my life*. New York: Doubleday, Page, & Co. Online Version retrieved from: http://www.etestingcenter.com/library/BooksJ-L/The%20Story%20of%20My%20Life.pdf

Kincheloe, J. (2008). *Critical pedagogy primer*. New York: Peter Lang.

Kliebard, H. (2004). *The struggle for the American curriculum 1893–1958*. New York: Routledge Falmer.

Kozulin, A. (1990). *Vygotsky's psychology: A biography of ideas*. Cambridge, MA: Harvard University Press.

Krashen, S. (1990). *Principles and practice in second language acquisition*. Upper Saddle River, NJ: Prentice-Hall.

Lakoff, G. & Johnson, M. (1980/2003). *Metaphors we live by*. Chicago: Chicago University Press.

Lakoff, G. & Johnson, M. (1999). *Philosophy in the flesh: The embodied mind and its challenge to Western thought*. New York: Basic Books.

Langford, P. E. (2005). *Vygotsky's developmental and educational psychology*. New York, NY: Psychology Press.

Lave, J., & Wenger, E. (1991). *Situated learning: Legitimate peripheral participation*. New York, NY: Cambridge University Press.

Lawton, D. (1984). Metaphor and the curriculum. In *Metaphors of Education*. (p. 79). W. Taylor (Ed.). London: Heinemann.

Louv, R. (2008). *Last child in the woods: Saving our children from nature deficit disorder*. Chapel Hill, NC. Algonquin Books of Chapel Hill.

Lowe, V. (2009). *Lev Vygotsky: One man's legacy through his life and theory*. [Motion picture]. Abbotsford, BC, Canada: PHD Lowe Productions.

Luria, A. R. (1979). *The making of mind: A personal account of soviet psychology*. Cambridge, MA: Harvard University Press.

Malott, C. (2011). *Critical Pedagogy and Cognition: An Introduction to a Postformal Educational Psychology*. New York. Springer.

Marx, Karl. (1997). *Preface to a contribution to the critique of political economy*. Trans. Rojas, R. Moscow: Progress Publishers. Retrieved from: http://www.marxists.org/archive/marx/works/1859/critique- pol-economy/preface.htm

Meshcheryakov, B. G. (2007). Terminology in L. S. Vygotsky's writings. In Daniels, H., Cole, M., Wertsch, J. V. (Eds.) *The Cambridge companion to Vygotsky*. New York, NY: Cambridge University Press.

Modell, A. (2003). *Imagination and the meaningful brain*. Boston: MIT Press.

Moffett, J. (1968). *Teaching the universe of discourse*. Boston: Houghton Mifflin.

Moll, L. C. (Ed.) (1990). *Vygotsky and education: Instructional implications and applications of sociohistorical psychology*. New York, NY: Cambridge University Press.

Moll, L. & Greenburg, J.B. (1990). Creating zones of possibilities: Combining social contexts for instruction. In Moll, L. C. (Ed.). *Vygotsky and education: Instructional implications and applications of sociohistorical psychology*. New York, NY: Cambridge University Press.

Moran, S., & John-Steiner, V. (2003). Creativity in the making: Vygotsky's contemporary contribution to the dialectic of development and creativity. In R. K. Sawyer, V. John-Steiner, S. Moran, R. J. Sternberg, D. H. Feldman, J. Nakamura, et al., *Creativity and development*. (pp. 61–90). New York: Oxford University Press.

Neil, M. (2011). *From the frying pan to the fire, while adding gasoline: Comments on, with excerpts from, the Education Department's ESEA/NCLB Waiver/Flexibility Provisions*. Retrieved from http://www.fairtest.org/sites/default/files/Fairtest_on_Waivers_092311.pdf

Newman, F., & Holtzman, L. (1993). *Lev Vygotsky: Revolutionary scientist*. London: Routledge.

Noddings, N.(1984). *Caring: A feminine approach to ethics and moral education*. Berkeley, CA. University of California Press

Oakeshott, M. (1962). *Rationalism in Politics and Other Essays*. London: Methuen.

Orman, M.(1995). *How Einstein arrived at E=MC2*. Retrieved from: http://www.stresscure.com/hrn/einstein.html

Pavlov, I. (1927). *Conditioned Reflexes*. Oxford: Oxford University Press.

Perry, T. B. (2005). Taking time: Beyond memorization: Using drama to promote thinking. *English Journal. 95.* (5).

Pinar, W. F. (2004). *What is curriculum theory?* Mahwah, NJ: Lawrence Erlbaum.

Richards, I. A. (1936). *The philosophy of rhetoric*. Oxford: Oxford University Press.

Richardson, L. (2003). Writing: A method of inquiry. In Denzin, N., & Lincoln, Y. (Eds.). *Collecting and interpreting qualitative materials*. (2nd ed., pp. 499–554). Thousand Oaks, CA: Sage.

Robbins, D. (2011). Vygotsky's ZPD interacting with American early childhood education. In C. Coreil (Ed). *The X point in education: Where imagination is lost.* Jersey City, NJ: New Jersey City University Press.

Roth, W., & Lee, Y. (2007). "Vygotsky's neglected legacy": Cultural-historical activity theory. *Review of Educational Research,* 77 (2), 186–232. doi: 10.3102/0034654306298273

Sacks, O. (1989). *Seeing voices: A journey into the world of the deaf.* Berkeley, CA: University of California Press.

Sandburg, C. (2001). Fog. *In Poetry Speaks.* p. 57. Naperville, IL: Sourcebooks.

Sawoski, P. (2011). *The Stanislavski System: Growth and Methodology*. Retrieved from: http://homepage.smc.edu/sawoski_perviz/Stanislavski.pdf

Schonert-Reichl, K.A. (2009). Research Report. *Roots of Empathy*. Retrieved from: http://www.rootsofempathy.org/documents/content/ROE_Report_Research_E_2009.pdf

Schubert, W., Schubert, A. L., Thomas, T., Carroll, W., & Forsyth, A. (2002). *Curriculum books: The first hundred years*. New York: Peter Lang.

Schwab, J. (1969). "The practical: A language for curriculum." *School Review,* 78(1): 1–23.

Schwab, J. (1978). *Science, curriculum, and liberal education: selected essays: Joseph J. Schwab.* Westbury, I., & Wilkof, N. J. (Eds.). Chicago: University of Chicago Press.

Share, J., Jolls, T, & Thoman, E. (2005). *Five key questions that can change the world.* Los Angeles, CA: Center for Media Literacy.

Sidorkin, A. M. (2002). *Learning relations: Impure education, deschooled school & dialogue with evil.* New York: Peter Lang.

Smidt, S. (2009). *Introducing Vygotsky: A guide for practitioners and students in early years education.* London: Routledge.

Stanislavsky, K. (1949). *Building a character.* New York: Theatre Arts Books.

Steinberg, S. (2011). *Kinderculture: The Corporate Construction of Childhood.* Boulder, CO: Westview Press.

Taylor, M., Carlson, S., Maring, B., Gerow, L., & Charley, C. (2004). The characteristics and correlates of fantasy in school- age children: Imaginary companions, impersonation, and social understanding. *Developmental Psychology,* Vol 40(6), Nov. 2004, pp. 1173–1187.

Thorndike, E. (1921). Measurement in education. *Teachers College Record,* XXII, 371–379.

Tobach, E., Falmagne, R. J., Parlee, M. B., Martin, L. M. W., & Kapelman, A. S. (Eds.) (1997). *Mind and social practice: Selected writings of Sylvia Scribner.* New York, NY: Cambridge University Press.

Trueba, E. T. (1999). Critical ethnography and a Vygotskian pedagogy of hope: The empowerment of Mexican immigrant children. *Qualitative Studies in Education, 12(6),* 591–614.

Valencia, R., & Solorzano, D. (1997). Contemporary Deficit Thinking. In R. Valencia (Ed.), *The Evolution of Deficit Thinking: Educational Thought and Practice.* (pp. 160–210). London, Washington, D.C.: Falmer Press.

Valenzuela, A. (1999). *Subtractive schooling. U.S.-Mexican youth and the politics of caring.* Albany, NY: State University of New York Press.

van der Veer, R. (n.d). *Early periods in the work of L.S. Vygotsky: The influence of Spinoza.* (Unpublished) Retrieved March 14, 2011, from: *https://openaccess.leidenuniv.nl/bitstream/1887/10217/1/7_703_038.pdf*

van der Veer, R. (1987). Review of *Thought and Langauge. The Journal of Mind and Behavior.* Vol. 8. No. 1, pp. 175–178.

van der Veer, R., & Valsiner, J. (1991). *Understanding Vygotsky: A quest for synthesis.* Cambridge, MA: Blackwell.

van der Veer, R., & Valsiner, J. (Eds.) (1994). *The Vygotsky reader.* Cambridge, MA: Blackwell.

Vasilyuk, F. (1988). *The psychology of experiencing.* Moscow: Progress Publishers.

Vico, G. (1744).*The new science.* Ithaca: Cornell University Press.

Vocate, D.R. (1994). Self-talk and inner speech. In D. Vocate (ed.). *Intrapersonal communication: Different voices, different minds.* Hillsdale, NJ: Lawrence Erlbaum.

Vygodskaya, G. (1995). His life. *School Psychology International.* Vol.16, No. 2, pp. 105–116.

Vygodsakaya, G. (1999). On Vygotsky's research and life. In S. Chaiklin, M. Hedegaard and U. J. Jensen (eds.) *Activity theory and social practice.* (pp. 31–38). Aarhus, Denmark: Aarhus University Press.

Vygotsky, L.S. (1925). *The psychology of art.* Retrieved from: http://www.marxists.org/archive/vygotsky/works/1925/art11.htm

Vygotsky, L. S. (1929). The problem of the cultural development of the child. *Journal of Genetic Psychology, 36,* 415–434.

Vygotsky, L. (1930/2004). Imagination and creativity in childhood. *Journal of Russian & East European Psychology, 42*(1), 7–97. Retrieved from EBSCO*host.*

Vygotsky, L. S. (1933/2002).*Play and its role in the Mental Development of the Child.* Retrieved June 14, 2011, from: Psychology and Marxism Internet Archive. marxists.org /archive/vygotsky/works/1933/play.htm

Vygotsky, L. S. (1962). *Thought and language.* Trans. E. Hanfman & V. Vakar. Cambridge, MA: MIT Press.

Vygotsky, L. S. (1978). *Mind in society: The development of higher psychological processes.* (M. Cole, V. John-Steiner, S. Scribner, & E. Souberman, Eds.). Cambridge, MA. Harvard University Press.

Vygotsky, L. S. 1981. The genesis of higher mental functions. In J. V. Wertsch (ed.), *The concept of activity in Soviet psychology.* Armonk, NY: Sharpe.

Vygotsky, L. S. (1982a). *Collected Works, Vol. 1.* Moscow: Pedagogika.

Vygotsky, L. S. (1982b). In lieu of an afterword. In Levitan, K. and Davydov, V. (Eds.), *One is not born a personality: Profiles of Soviet educational psychologists.* (pp. 11–20). Moscow: Progress Publishers.

Vygotsky, L. S. 1986. *Thought and language.* Trans. A. Kozulin. Cambridge, MA: MIT Press.

Vygotsky, L. S. (1987a). The problem of speech and thinking in Piaget's theory. In R. W. Rieber & A. S. Carton (Eds.), *Collected works of L. S. Vygotsky: Vol. 1. Problems of general psychology.* (pp. 53–91). New York: Plenum. (Original work published 1934).

Vygotsky, L. S. (1987b).The genetic roots of thinking and speaking. In R. W. Rieber & A. S. Carton (Eds.), *Collected works of L. S. Vygotsky: Vol. 1. Problems of general psychology* (pp. 101–120). New York: Plenum. (Original work published 1934).

Vygotsky, L. S. (1987c). An experimental study of concept development. In R. W. Rieber & A. S. Carton (Eds.), *Collected works of L. S. Vygotsky: Vol. 1. Problems of general psychology* (pp. 121–166). New York: Plenum. (Original work published (1934).

Vygotsky, L. S. (1987d). The development of scientific concepts in childhood. In R. W. Rieber & A. S. Carton (Eds.), *Collected works of*

L. S. Vygotsky: Vol. 1. Problems of general psychology (pp. 167–241). New York: Plenum. (Original work published in 1934).

Vygotsky, L. S. (1987e). Thought and word. In R. W. Rieber & A. S. Carton (Eds.), *Collected works of L. S. Vygotsky: Vol. 1. Problems of general psychology* (pp. 243–288). New York: Plenum. (Original work published 1934).

Vygotsky, L. S. (1987f). Thinking and its development in childhood. In R. W. Rieber & A. S. Carton (Eds.), *Collected works of L. S. Vygotsky: Vol. 1. Problems of general psychology* (pp. 311–324). New York: Plenum. (Original work published 1934).

Vygotsky, L. S. (1993). In R. W. Rieber (Ed.), *Collected works of L. S. Vygotsky: Vol. 2. The fundamentals of defectology (The diagnostics of development and the pedological clinic for difficult children).* (pp. 241–292). New York: Plenum.

Vygotsky, L. S. (1994a). The problem of environment. In R. van der Veer and J. Valsiner (Eds.), *The Vygotsky reader* (pp. 338–354). Oxford: Blackwell Press.

Vygotsky, L. S. (1994b). The development of thinking and concept formation in adolescence. In R. van der Veer & J. Valsiner (Eds.), *The Vygotsky reader* (pp. 185–265). Oxford: Blackwell Press.

Vygotsky, L. S. (1994c). "The socialist alteration of man." In R. van der Veer & J. Valsiner (Eds.). *The Vygotsky reader.* (pp. 175–184). Oxford: Blackwell Press.

Vygotsky, L. S. (1997a). The instrumental method in psychology. In R. W. Rieber & J. Wollock (Eds.), *Collected works of L. S. Vygotsky: Vol. 3. Problems of the theory and history of psychology* (pp. 85–89). New York: Plenum. (Original work published 1982–1984)

Vygotsky, L. S. (1997b). On psychological systems. In R. W. Rieber & J. Wollock (Eds.), *Collected works of L. S. Vygotsky: Vol. 3. Problems of the theory and history of psychology* (pp. 91–107). (Original work published 1982–1984)

Vygotsky, L. S. (1997c). The historical meaning of the crisis in psychology: A methodological investigation. In R. W. Rieber & J. Wollock (Eds.), *Collected works of L. S. Vygotsky: Vol. 3. Problems of the theory and history of psychology* (pp. 233–244). (Original work published 1982–1984).

Vygotsky, L. S. (1997d). Research method. In R. W. Rieber (Ed.), *Collected works of L. S. Vygotsky: Vol. 4. The history of the development of higher mental functions* (pp. 27–63). New York: Plenum. (Original work published 1960).

Vygotsky, L. S. (1997e). Analysis of higher mental functions. In R. W. Rieber (Ed.), *Collected works of L. S. Vygotsky: Vol. 4. The history of*

the development of higher mental functions (pp. 65–82). New York: Plenum. (Original work published 1960).

Vygotsky, L. S. (1997f). Conclusion; further research; development of personality and world view in the child. In R. Rieber (Ed.), *Collected works of L. S. Vygotsky: Vol. 4. The history of the development of higher mental functions* (pp. 241–251). New York: Plenum. (Original work published in 1982–1984).

Vygotsky, L. S. (1998a). Development of the higher mental functions during the transitional age. In R. W. Rieber (Ed.), *Collected works of L. S. Vygotsky: Vol. 5. Child psychology* (pp. 83–149). New York: Plenum. (Original work published 1930–1931)

Vygotsky, L. S. (1998b). Imagination and creativity in the adolescent. In R. W. Rieber (Ed.), *Collected works of L. S. Vygotsky: Vol. 5. Child psychology* (pp. 166–184). New York: Plenum. (Original work published 1930–1931).

Vygotsky, L. S. (1998c). Early childhood. In R. W. Rieber (Ed.), *Collected works of L. S. Vygotsky: Vol. 5. Child psychology* (pp. 261–281). New York: Plenum. (Original work published 1982–1984).

Vygotsky, L. S. (1998d). The problem of age. In R. W. Rieber (Ed.), *Collected works of L. S. Vygotsky: Vol. 5. Child psychology* (pp. 184–205). New York: Plenum. (Original work published 1982–1984).

Vygotsky, L. S. (1999). Analysis of sign operations of the child. In R. W. Rieber (Ed.), *Scientific legacy* (pp. 45–56). New York: Plenum. (Original work published 1982–1984).

Vygotsky, L. S., & Luria, A. R. (1993). *Studies in the history of behavior: Ape, primitive, and child.* Hillsdale, NJ: Erlbaum. (Original work published 1930).

Vygotsky, L. S., & Luria, A. R. (1994). Tool and symbol in child development. In R. van der Veer & J. Valsiner (Eds.), *The Vygotsky reader* (pp. 99–174). Cambridge, MA: Blackwell.

Wellings, P. (2003). *Vygotsky: School learning ver&sus Life learning: The interaction of spontaneous & scientific concepts in the development of higher mental processes.* Unpublished paper. Retrieved from: http://ldt.stanford.edu/~paulaw/STANFORD/370x_paula_wellings_final_paper.pdf

Wertsch, J. V. (1985). *Vygotsky and the social formation of mind.* Cambridge, MA: Harvard University Press.

Wertsch, J. V. (1991). *Voices of the mind: A sociocultural approach to mediated action.* Cambridge, MA: Harvard University Press.

Wink, J. & Putney, L. (2003). *A vision of Vygotsky.* Boston, MA: Allyn & Bacon.

Zebroski, J. T. (1994). *Thinking through theory: Vygotskian perspectives on the teaching of writing.* Portsmouth, NH: Boynton/Cook Publishers, Inc.

Resources for Vygotskian Practice

Vygotsky Documentary—Abbotsford, BC, Canada: PHD Lowe Productions.

From the website: *Lev Vygotsky: One man's legacy through his life and practice* explores the compelling story of this father of Russian psychology. This documentary uses a mixture of interviews and commentary from family members Gita L. Vygodskaya and Elena Kravtzova, renowned professors-educators including Michael Cole, Lois Holzman, Vera John-Steiner, Alex Kozulin, Tamara Lifanova, Luciano Mecacci, James Wertsch, and others; archive photos, film footage, narration; and Vygotskian practice examples. Retrieved from: http://www.vygotskydocumentary.com

Tools of the Mind—Denver, Colorado, USA

From their website: The concept of "Tools of the Mind" comes from the work of Russian psychologist Lev Vygotsky, He believed that just as physical tools extend our physical abilities, mental tools extend our mental abilities to enable us to solve problems and create solutions in the modern world. According to Vygotsky, until children learn to use mental tools, their learning is largely controlled by the environment: they attend only to the things that are the brightest or loudest and they can remember something only if has been repeated many times. After children master mental tools, they can become in charge of their own learning by attending and remembering in an intentional and purposeful way. Similar to how using mental tools transforms children's cognitive behaviors, they can also transform their physical, social and emotional behaviors. From being "slaves to the environment," children become "masters of their own behavior." As children are taught and practice an increasing number of various mental tools, they transform not only their external behaviors but also their minds, leading to the emergence of higher mental functions. Retrieved from: http://www.mscd.edu/extendedcampus/toolsofthemind/about/index.shtml

The Met—Providence, Rhode Island, USA

From their website: The MET is a network of six small, public high schools located in Providence and Newport, Rhode Island. With high standards and strong family engagement, the MET's individualized learning approach has proven successful in unlocking students' passion for learning. The MET empowers its students to take

charge of their learning, to become responsible citizens and life-long learners. The hallmarks of a MET education include internships, individual learning plans, advisory, and a breakthrough college transition program. The MET is the model for 80 schools across the country. It is the leader in school reform and is consistently identified by a sweeping range of education leaders as one of the most effective models in the country.

The MET is a state-funded public school district and our educators are certified teachers committed to doing what's best for kids. Retrieved from: http://metcenter.org/about-us/

The Roots of Empathy—Toronto, Ontario, Canada

From their website: In the Roots of Empathy program, a parent and baby (who is two to four months old at the start of the program) from the community visit a classroom nine times over the course of a school year. A trained Roots of Empathy instructor visits with the family to guide children as they observe the relationship between the baby and his or her parent. The instructor also visits before and after each family visit to reinforce teachings. There are 27 classroom visits in total in a Roots of Empathy program. In the program, the baby is the "teacher." With each family visit, the instructor leads the children in noticing how the baby is growing and changing over the course of his or her first year of life. Retrieved from: http://www.rootsofempathy.org/en/who-we-are/about-roots-of-empathy.html

The 5th Dimension—San Diego California, USA

From their website: The 5th Dimension was established in the 1980s as a partnership between community centers and local colleges to establish an educational after-school program. With an emphasis on diversity and computer technology, the program incorporates the latest theories about child development and gives college students the opportunity to apply their textbook understanding of child development to real learning environments. The 5th Dimension explores the design, implementation, and evaluation of this thriving program. The authors attribute the success of the 5th Dimension to several factors. First, the program offers a balance of intellectually enriching exercises with development enhancing games. Second, by engaging undergraduates as active participants in both learning and social activities, the program gives local community organizations a large infusion of high-quality help for their educational efforts. Third, by rewarding children for their achievements and good behavior with greater flexibility in choosing their own schedules, the 5th Dimension acts as a powerful, enduring motivator. Retrieved from: http://5thd.communication.ucsd.edu/Startmenu.htm

The East Side Institute—New York City, New York, USA

From their website: The East Side Institute is an international non-profit which for nearly three decades has functioned as an independent research, training and organizing center at the forefront of new approaches to human development, learning, therapeutics and community building. Since the mid-1980s, the Institute has evolved a social-cultural approach to human development that relates to people of all ages as performers and creators of their lives. Our approach—social therapy—is at once a group-oriented, development-focused psychotherapy and a methodology with broad application in educational, cultural, health and community settings. Social therapy is practiced at seven social therapy centers in the US. Over the last three decades, the Institute has introduced cutting-edge approaches to human development and learning to tens of thousands of people in the U.S. and throughout the world. Retrieved from: http://www.eastsideinstitute.org

The Center for Research on Activity, Development and Learning—Helsinki, Finland

From their website: We are a multidisciplinary research unit, focused on transformations and learning in collective activity systems and individuals facing new societal, cultural and technological challenges. Our work is inspired by cultural-historical activity theory and more broadly socio-cultural approaches to human development. We are a community of researchers based at University of Helsinki. Our research is based on interplay between theory and practice. We work in close collaboration with various work organizations, educational institutions, and other communities of practice. Much of our research uses formative interventions, such as Change Laboratories. We are part of a growing international network of research groups which share a similar theoretical approach. In our Center, we have a good number of research projects as well as a doctoral program and a Master's program. Retrieved from: http://www.helsinki.fi/cradle/index.htm

International Center for the Enhancement of Learning Potential—Jerusalem, Israel

From their website: The International Center for the Enhancement of Learning Potential (ICELP) was established with the goal of continuing and expanding the educational and psychological work initiated by Prof. Feuerstein. The work of the ICELP is based on the theories of Structural Cognitive Modifiability and Mediated Learning Experience, which serve as a basis for three applied systems: the Learning Potential Assessment Device (LPAD), Instrumental Enrichment (IE) cognitive intervention program, and Shaping Modifying Environment. ICELP specializes in providing a

wide range of services, trainings, research and development. Retrieved from: http://www.icelp.org/asp/main.asp

The Research Center for Developmental Teaching and Learning—Kajaani, Finland

From their website: The Center for Developmental Teaching and Learning was founded in 1999. The ultimate goal is to study and reveal moving forces and laws of cultural development. This goal is divided into sub goals such as elaboration of the concept and models of cultural development, social situations of development, activity systems, and interrelations between education, learning and development. Our main focuses of research are developmental trajectories and qualitative systemic transitions. According to the dynamic theory of psychological age in cultural-historical approach we separate functional and age-related development from each other. Most research programs operate with theoretically understood age concept. The center takes the task of elaborating the methodology for studying developmental processes in different environments and stages of life. A springboard in this work will be the method of genetic and natural experiments introduced in cultural-historical psychology. Experimental work is supported with the elaboration of the basic genetic law of human development and the zones of proximal development. Retrieved from: http://www.kajaaninyliopistokeskus.oulu.fi/tutkimuskonsortio/developunit.htm

The Mind, Culture, and Activity Homepage—San Diego, California, USA

From their website: The *Mind, Culture, and Activity Homepage* is an interactive forum for a community of interdisciplinary scholars who share an interest in the study of human mind in its cultural and historical contexts. Our emphasis is research that seeks to resolve methodological problems associated with the analysis of human and theoretical approaches that place culture and activity at the center of attempts to understand human nature. Our participants come from a variety of disciplines, including anthropology, cognitive science, education, linguistics, psychology and sociology. Central to the organization of activities in the community is the **Laboratory of Comparative Human Cognition** at the University of California, San Diego. LCHC publishes the Mind, Culture, and Activity journal (MCA) and sponsors XMCA, an e-mail discussion group. This homepage seeks to integrate a variety of activities in the community into one on-line resource. On this page you will find links to current and past issues of MCA, on-line discussions from the XMCA mailing list, personal profiles of our participants, and links to other related Web sites. Retrieved from: http://lchc.ucsd.edu/mca/

Index

Peter Lang
PRIMERS
in Education

Peter Lang Primers are designed to provide a brief and concise introduction or supplement to specific topics in education. Although sophisticated in content, these primers are written in an accessible style, making them perfect for undergraduate and graduate classroom use. Each volume includes a glossary of key terms and a References and Resources section.

Other published and forthcoming volumes cover such topics as:

- Standards
- Popular Culture
- Critical Pedagogy
- Literacy
- Higher Education
- John Dewey
- Feminist Theory and Education
- Studying Urban Youth Culture
- Multiculturalism through Postformalism
- Creative Problem Solving
- Teaching the Holocaust
- Piaget and Education
- Deleuze and Education
- Foucault and Education

Look for more Peter Lang Primers to be published soon. To order other volumes, please contact our Customer Service Department:

800-770-LANG (within the US)
212-647-7706 (outside the US)
212-647-7707 (fax)

To find out more about this and other Peter Lang book series, or to browse a full list of education titles, please visit our website:
www.peterlang.com